COBS CAN!

COBS CAN!

Training and Riding the Versatile Cob

OMAR RABIA

J.A. ALLEN · LONDON

© Omar Rabia 2011
First published in Great Britain in 2011
Reprinted 2011, 2012 and 2013

ISBN 978 0 85131 976 6

J. A. Allen
Clerkenwell House
Clerkenwell Green
London EC1R OHT

J.A. Allen is an imprint of Robert Hale Limited

www.allenbooks.co.uk

A catalogue record for this book is available from the British Library

Designed and typeset by Paul Saunders
Edited by Martin Diggle
Photographs by/courtesy of Jesse Ambridge, David Harrison,
Sam Jamieson, Laura Baird, Clare Barlow and Lynn Russell
Diagrams by Carole Vincer; line drawings by Jennifer Bell

Printed by Craft Print International Limited, Singapore

Contents

Acknowledgements

The acknowledgements have been far harder to write than a lot of this book. I have been desperate not to leave anyone out because, without everyone's help, I couldn't have done this. My first thanks have to go to my grandparents Bob and Ivy Fisher. They started me off on my equestrian journey and indeed bought my first cob, Habeabtie. It's just a shame neither of them is here to see my project come to fruition, therefore I am dedicating this book to them. I would also like to thank my partner Ian and my family (especially my mother Jean, and my sister Zako) for their support, especially when I was ready to give up! My very good friends Anne and Sandra need special mention also because of their encouragement and astute observations – thank you. My pupils and clients Sarah Fell, Nicola Myers, Caroline Breeze and Ann Sewell, who have helped me in the writing and illustrating of this book, of course need recognition; I couldn't have taken on this task without their support. I must thank the following friends, fellow instructors and trainers for their help in illustrating this book: Sam Jamieson, Lucie Evans, Janice Hutchinson and Helen Waine all gave their time freely for photo shoots, often at very short notice. I would also like to thank Lynn Russell for her photos which bring a showing perspective to parts of the book. Thanks to Martin Diggle for his tireless editing of my work; he was able to turn my words into those that could be understood by anyone. Thanks to the illustrators Carole Vincer and Jennifer Bell for producing the diagrams and line drawings which help to bring parts of the book to life. A great big thanks to the photographers Jesse Ambridge, David Harrison and Laura Baird for their work. Thanks to David for dropping everything at a moment's notice and Laura for being a perfectionist in looking for just the right shot. Finally a huge thank you to Lesley Gowers for seeing the potential in my work and taking a risk on *Cobs Can!* Thank you all.

Introduction

Cobs are either loved or loathed by the great riding public. They have earned the reputation of being a steady, confidence-giving ride. They have earned the reputation in some quarters for being a good fun ride, but they are also thought of by many as being lazy, stubborn, heavy and stiff. I feel that this latter reputation is a result of a number of factors, mostly down to the riders, certainly not because of the cobs themselves. A lot of cobs are ridden by nervous riders who prefer a slower mount; often because of this these people do not ride their cobs forward in the mistaken belief that it may excite them. Some, also, are ridden by stiffer riders who are reassured by their smaller stature, and as a result of the rider's stiffness the cob's suppleness can be impaired. Cobs are often reserved for first-time owners and as a result of the rider's lack of experience, the cob is not schooled to his optimum. What I am *not* saying is that these animals should not be ridden by these people. Indeed, these wonderful creatures are ideally suited to these situations because of their superb and caring temperaments, their steady nature and way of going and, of course, their reassuring stature. What I *am* saying is let's not think that that's all a cob has to offer.

I believe that each of the situations mentioned above has contributed to the negative views some people hold about the cob. However, I also believe the fact that cobs are thought of as steady enough and gentle enough for novice, stiff or elderly riders only goes to show

their true generous nature and amazing temperaments. If so allowed, a cob will be forward, attentive, light, supple and incredibly agile.

I have decided to write this book as a celebration of these fantastic creatures. I am hoping that, as a result of this book, people may stop thinking that their riding ability has outgrown their cob and that some may consider owning a lovely cob rather than going out and buying a sports horse. I am also hoping to show the riding teachers, dressage trainers and judges just how capable cobs are and how well they can work. I am hoping that cobs will gain the appreciation of the powers that be, so that those who choose to compete on cobs gain deserved recognition from judges and trainers alike.

I would also like to emphasize, to both riders and trainers, the point that there are certain techniques for schooling cobs which are more successful than some of the modern methods used for other breeds and types, especially Warmbloods/sports horses. I want to show a training method that is suitable for cobs and horses of heavier stature as these animals rarely respond optimally to modern dressage training techniques. Cobs are capable of all the movements performed by these Warmbloods/sports horses, but there are visual differences related to their conformation. For example, they can truly collect – it just looks different; they can truly extend – it just looks different. My aim is to point out these areas so that their work is acknowledged as being correct.

Although my main aim is to illustrate cobs' capabilities (not necessarily to produce a training manual), I have included all the methods that I use to train my cobs. Regarding the point just mentioned, I felt I needed to illustrate, for example, the fact that cobs don't go so well if ridden too forwards and that some alternatives may be worth investigating. However, I want to make it clear that these methods are not 'my methods' but are tried and tested methods often thought of as 'classical' techniques. I hope that, as a result of this book, I can challenge commonly held misconceptions about the typical cob, and that in the future I will hear fewer comments such as 'common cob' and 'numb cob' and will hear, instead, more of a celebration of these wonderful creatures.

Intelligence, character and a biddable nature are all shown here.

My passion for the cob started when I took my sister at the age of 10 to look for her first pony. We visited a dealer who had a variety of cobs available. We looked at a couple of hopefuls, and then a lovely skewbald mare emerged from the crowd. There wasn't anything particularly special about the way she looked but the moment she was tacked up and ridden it became more than apparent that she was the one. Ketchup (so named because she was quite orange and looked like a white horse who had been splattered with tomato sauce) could be hacked up and down slip roads with huge juggernauts passing her on main carriageways without flinching. At first, she could shuffle in walk, she could trot (trot was most definitely her natural gait!) but canter just wasn't in her repertoire. Nevertheless she was perfect! Of course I continued her education in between my sister's rides and gradually, as my sister lost interest, I took over responsibility for Ketchup. I just couldn't bare the thought of selling her; she was just the nicest 'person' with a great attitude.

At the time, I owned a part-bred Trakehner gelding, Taz, whom I competed in affiliated dressage competitions. I was ignorant of the real capabilities of cobs and wanted a 'competition horse' – which of course had to be a sports horse or a Warmblood. Taz was a great educator and really put me through my paces. He was a confirmed rearer, and often

Show cobs have long been appreciated by the showing fraternity. Here Lynn Russell shows how stunning a show cob can be when turned out in side-saddle.

put me in my place by giving a good buck. But he won rosettes and points, so I put up with it. At the same time, Ketchup's education continued and it wasn't that long before I realized that she could do some of the more fancy lateral work that was often seen as the province of Warmbloods in the dressage arena. It dawned on me that, actually, riding her was a lot more fun. She was and is by far the most consistent horse I have ever ridden. Ketchup is now approaching Advanced level. She is capable of all the lateral work, in all gaits. She has developed a correct, rhythmical, expressive piaffe and, at the time of writing, is on the way to developing a lovely active passage. She needs to start developing her flying changes and her canter pirouettes.

Ketchup has most certainly changed my attitude towards lovely cobs and their capabilities. One instructor once said, 'Cobs can't but Ketchup can!' and I want to retort by saying, 'No! Cobs genuinely can!' As a result of this book I want to hear fewer trainers and judges saying things like, 'Well, if you are genuinely serious about dressage then you are starting with the wrong raw material.' Remember, the fact is that dressage was made for horses (cobs and ponies included), not that horses (by which many think Warmbloods) were made for dressage!

Although this book is primarily about cobs, I think and believe that the methods herein would suit any native type of pony as well as any other heavier stamp of horse. They would work well with British and other native types of pony such as the Austrian Haflinger, the Norwegian Fjord and the Icelandic, as well as with horses such as the Clydesdale, Cleveland Bay, Irish Draught and the Continental draught horses. I have tried, where possible, to include photos of such horses and ponies as evidence.

Through this book I hope to show that cobs can compete alongside their Warmblood counterparts quite successfully.

....

CHAPTER ONE

A Cob's Qualities

Conformation

Let's take a closer look at a typical cob. It is conformation that makes an animal a 'cob' rather than a horse or a pony. A cob is usually quite short in stature, usually less than 15.3hh, but I believe this book is relevant to any horse of heavy build irrespective of actual height. A cob usually has a deep girth, short, strong and well-built legs, a short, strong back and a medium length of neck which is well muscled and well arched. In this chapter I will discuss the different parts of a cob in more detail and point out various strengths and weaknesses that may be evident in a typical riding cob.

Head

It has been said that a cob 'should have a head like a lady's maid and the backside of a cook'. I think this is a great description. A cob should have an attractive head which is neither too heavy nor too fine for his overall conformation. Such a head is usually wide between the eyes – an attribute that some people feel is a feature that denotes intelligence. The head tapers slightly to the muzzle and the overall length of the head should not be too long. On occasion, a cob may have a head that looks too big and coarse for his overall conformation. I don't believe that a large, coarse head really affects the overall performance capability of the cob, except that it can sometimes inhibit the cob from assuming an

Here the Friesian stallion Liuwe shows impressive presence, and a fantastic shoulder. In the flesh Liuwe is magnificent, awesome even. It's amazing how stallions like Liuwe simply exude quality, presence and masculine power. His gaits are airborne and his temperament is excellent.

entirely 'uphill' way of going. There is, of course, the aesthetic factor, but isn't every horse beautiful in his own way? Far more important to the cob's capability is the way the head is set onto the neck.

Neck

The cob's head should join onto the neck in such a way that he will be able to flex sufficiently at the poll, so that the head approaches a vertical plane without the jowl restricting this flexion. The jowl is on the underside where the head joins the neck, often described as the throat. When viewed from the side the jowl should not be too thick. Horses with this type of conformation can often look 'stuffy' in outline (and feel so when ridden), but if you make sure there is enough stretch over the topline, it is still possible to develop a good outline. Cobs with coarse jowls can go correctly but extra care must be taken to make sure that they do not get too stuffy, short-striding or strong. If they are ridden too forward, as is often the case in modern dressage training methods, these cobs will turn into heavy tanks, ploughing through your hands. If you are not observant in this area, and you ride your cob with a short, tight neck, cobs with jowly conformation can have problems with painfully crushed parotid glands. If there isn't sufficient clearance between the jaw bones and the first and second cervical vertebrae then, when the rider pulls the cob into a short outline, he compresses the parotid glands between the jaw and the leading edge of the cervical vertebrae, causing considerable pain.

The neck itself is usually of a medium length, well curved and fairly well muscled. A weakness most often seen in cobs is a short, thick neck, which makes it easier for the cob to 'contract' his neck and become

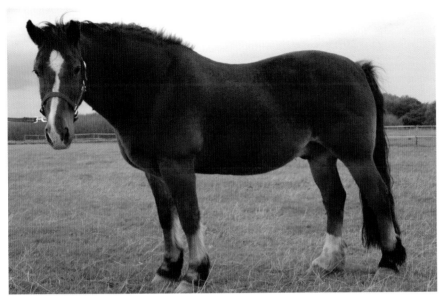

King is a lovely stamp of cob. He looks as if he has native (probably Welsh) blood. He has a lovely front with a nicely shaped neck which comes out of his shoulders well and connects to his head well for dressage. He has a good length of croup and nice limbs. He is maybe just a little bit on the long side in his loins.

Lucky is very different from King. She is a much heavier type of cob and stands a little back at the knee. She has a moderate length of neck and back and is well-balanced, although she stands a little croup-high. Her head-carriage is much higher than King's, which is of great advantage in more advanced dressage work.

strong in the hand, or fall onto the forehand and lean on the rider's hands. If your cob has this type of conformation don't despair, just take care! The moment he gets too low, pushes onto your hands or speeds up, do something about it, such as raising your hands, slowing the tempo of your rhythm, putting a little extra tone into the muscles of your torso and keep your legs encouraging a deeper placement of the hind legs (without rushing the movement more forward with extra speed) and soon your cob will be 'uphill', light and in self-carriage. Most cobs do, in fact, have sufficient length of rein. However, another point that is important is how the neck is set onto the shoulder and the angle of the shoulder itself (see below).

Shoulder

A cob's shoulder is usually set at a moderate angle, that is to say, not the same sloping angle typical of a Warmblood or Thoroughbred, but certainly not as upright as may be typical of many carriage horse breeds. An upright shoulder has an adverse effect on a horse's movement; it makes the steps shorter, a little higher, with more knee action and slightly more jarring for both horse and rider. An upright shoulder will have less range of movement than a more sloping shoulder, but correct schooling can help considerably. Horses with upright shoulders will

Ketchup, the inspiration of this book and certainly the best teacher anyone could ask for. Ketchup has very good conformation. Good enough, in fact, to qualify in the traditional cob class to go to the Championships at Stoneleigh. She has a nice short back and a moderate length of neck, which is well-shaped and set high – ideal for advanced dressage movements. Her quarters are moderately sized and well rounded in shape. She is blessed with wonderful limbs.

never lengthen extravagantly but with schooling they can become smoother in their action and can certainly lengthen and stride out to the extent that their conformation permits, provided the rider allows it. A moderately sloping shoulder, more typical of a cob, has a greater range of movement than just described and allows a smoother natural stride and a more favourable length of step.

The neck needs to 'grow' gracefully out of the shoulder, arching towards the poll. With most cobs this is true, and this allows the cob to work more easily in a correct outline, keeping the shoulders mobile. Sometimes a cob's neck is set on rather low and often looks as though the neck is 'stuck on the front'. This conformation is made more difficult if combined with the more upright shoulder as it makes it harder for the cob to 'come up and round'. It is all too easy for such a cob to contract his neck, lean on the rider's hands and get strong. For cobs with this conformation, diligence from the rider is the key.

Spike is a gorgeous, generous cob. I knew him while he was living with a previous owner, and he is the perfect horse for his current owner Andrea. Spike has been blessed with great limbs, a lovely long neck and a kind eye. His only failing is that he has quite a short, sloping croup but this does not affect his hind leg action.

Barrel and back

In these areas we rarely have a problem with our typical cob as usually they have a short, compact back which is strong and well muscled. The cob is usually deep through the girth, which gives plenty of heart room and scope for lung expansion. The typical short length and strength of a cob's back is an asset; however it can sometimes come with its own slight drawbacks. Sometimes horses with a shorter, stronger back can be a little tighter through this region than those with a slightly longer one, and sometimes such animals can actually tighten their back against the rider. However, I believe this can often be as a result of the way they are ridden rather than the fact that they have short backs. If the riding technique is less than favourable, cobs with shorter backs are more able to escape the consequent discomfort than their slightly longer-backed counterparts.

Haunches and hindquarters

Behind the saddle, as it were, are the cob's haunches. If we discuss these (without discussing the legs as yet) we will usually use words such as 'well-rounded', 'full' and 'well-muscled'. Cobs' quarters are usually fairly well sloped rather than straight, as is often the case with some Warm-blood strains. These qualities are big advantages for a riding horse. Well-structured quarters make it easy for a cob to collect sufficiently, to flex in the hip and stifle and to round the back into the collected movements. With the haunches positioned in such a way, the cob will therefore be able to lengthen expressively into a well-cadenced medium or extended gait. In some cobs, however, the quarters are extremely short and are excessively sloped. This can actually serve to tighten the cob in the back and does limit the range of movement in the hind legs in much the same way as an upright shoulder does with the forelegs. It is a common misconception that this type of conformation is advantageous in schooling for and performance of correct collection. However, as with a straight shoulder, this does not preclude such an animal from benefiting from correct schooling as long as sufficient thought is given to how this is carried out.

Legs and feet

A cob's legs have got to be his greatest strength. The limbs have sufficient quality of bone, are well made, with sufficiently short cannon bones, well-muscled forearms and thighs and, of course, well-formed and mobile joints. Cobs' hooves are almost without exception well shaped and with good-quality, hard-wearing horn.

Conformation considerations for showing

If showing is your first aim and you are looking for a new partner then conformation is a priority. There are now many classes for the cob but each section has its own requirements. For example what is required of a 'show cob' is quite different from a 'traditional cob' and they in turn are different from 'vanner cobs'.

Show cobs need outstanding conformation because all entrants are hogged and trimmed. This means you cannot hide weaker areas such as thick jowls and cow hocks. Show cobs generally have a medium length of neck, moderately sloping shoulders, a short, strong back and well-rounded, shapely quarters. In terms of bone these cobs need at least 9 in (bone is traditionally measured in inches – approx. 23cm) to qualify for the lightweight cob class. Show cobs should have an attractive, workmanlike head. A highly refined head would look out of place though as mentioned earlier there is a saying that a good cob should have a 'head like a duchess and the bottom of a cook'.

Show cobs traditionally have stood between 14.2hh and 15.1hh, though now we have maxi-cob classes starting at 15.2hh with no upper height limit. Conversely, there is also a modern tendency to breed them smaller and smaller and there is a fashion to have them as small as

Glen is a huge horse, at least 17.2hh and not easy to ride. At first glance many would say he is not a cob but he is a heavy, broad chap and definitely needs to be ridden as outlined in this book. Were he 15hh, no one would argue that he wasn't a cob. He is blessed with good conformation and movement.

12.2hh! Ketchup is classed as a traditional cob. She stands 14.2hh and has pretty much ideal conformation for these classes.

Traditional cobs are generally coloured in the tobiano or sabino pattern and indeed in the show ring the more attractively marked coloured specimens do very well indeed. Coloured cobs with a basic shield around the flanks on either side are generally marked down in

Victor is a purebred Clydesdale gelding, 17hh. His conformation is typically Clydesdale: his neck is long and fairly low-set, his shoulder is moderately angled but fairly long. He has good quarters for a Clydesdale, being well rounded (some of the breed have short, sloping quarters). His hind legs are a little close together as is typical of the breed, and he does dish a little. He is a very active chap and very capable.

Presented as a show cob, Wizard does very well in that role – as you can see, his conformation is excellent. His limbs are excellent and his movement is wonderful. He is as close to perfection as you can get!

respect of colour beside cobs marked like Ketchup. Poorly marked traditional cobs can win, however, if their conformation is outstanding compared to other entrants. Conformation comes first; colour would be the deciding factor when two equally good cobs come together. As distinct from show cobs, traditional cobs are shown with full, very long manes, full tails and full, thick feather. The more quality feather the better!

A vanner is usually a bigger type of cob, standing 15.2hh or more. They often appear leggier than the traditional cob, usually because of an infusion of Clydesdale blood. Vanners are often placed in traditional cob classes, which is a shame because they do not always meet the standard of points for the traditional cob. CHAPS (Coloured Horse and Pony Society) have an individual standard for the vanner.

Smokey is a lovely chap to work with. He is very chunky, with huge breadth between his forelegs and also his hips. He is blessed with good conformation, although he could have a slightly longer neck and a slightly more sloping shoulder. His attitude is good and his movement is great, with fantastic rhythm.

Tack to suit cobs' conformation

It is important for any horse that the tack used is chosen with reference to conformation. I usually keep things a simple as possible when choosing tack suitable for my cobs.

Saddles

Because most cobs have massive shoulders, low withers and short backs, a straighter-cut saddle such a dressage, working hunter or VSD style saddle is most suitable. In a treed saddle this keeps the points of the saddle further back behind the shoulders, giving greater freedom of movement. Because dressage is a major interest of mine, I usually use dressage saddles on my cobs. If jumping is your thing then a working hunter or VSD saddle should be more suitable for you than a dressage version.

I now use treeless saddles on all of my horses, including my cobs. I have found that many saddlers tend to fit treed saddles too narrow and this resulted in Ketchup needing regular back treatment both from vets and osteopaths. Since I switched to treeless, I've found that Ketchup now needs only 'MOT' type treatments on an annual basis.

Aside from their impact on the horse, I've found that some saddle designs restrict rider movement and inhibit the rider from easily adopting the classical position. This is often because the stirrup bars are far too far forward. In this position the stirrups actually pull the rider's legs much too far forward. This is exacerbated by the fact that many saddles have very narrow, hard twists, which encourage the rider to sit more on the 'back pockets' rather than upright and on the seat bones. When deciding on a saddle, choose one in which the stirrup bars are set further back. Make sure it is wide enough on your cob, so that it doesn't pinch and doesn't restrict the movement of the shoulders. When viewed from the side, the deepest part of the saddle should be in the middle. If it is too far back, it will put you behind the movement, while if it is too far forward it is likely to sit you on your fork and put you in front of the movement.

The treeless models that I use have been intelligently designed with a lot of these points taken into consideration. I use the same design on all of my horses and balance them as necessary. They are designed to allow freedom through the horse's shoulders and sit the rider in the

A treeless saddle, which may be suitable for cobs. I have used this saddle on Ketchup and she loved the feeling. She felt very free and supple in it, probably because there are no tree points that could inhibit her shoulders. It is more difficult to sit in the shoulder–hip–heel alignment because it doesn't have a built up twist to accommodate a rider's 'A' frame.

My dressage saddle. It is an Enlightened Equitation Fhoenix (yes, that is how it's spelt) saddle. With this saddle you have the advantages of a treeless saddle not inhibiting the shoulders, and the built up twist that will help the shoulder–hip–heel alignment. This saddle has a 'smart panel', which is basically a bean bag that distributes any pressure caused.

Another Enlightened Equitation Fhoenix saddle. This one with Prolite panels instead of the 'smart panel'.

A popular treed GP saddle. This one isn't particularly forward cut, which is just about perfect to fit a cob with big shoulders. With these saddles you need to make sure they are wide enough for your cob because you don't want the tree points to put pressure on your cob's shoulders.

Many would call this a 'floating panel' saddle. It was designed by friends who felt traditional saddles were inadequate for endurance riding. They have used them on their Icelandic horses and find them invaluable. The floating panels move and mould to the contours and movement of the horse and allow for great freedom of movement in the shoulders.

An old jumping saddle, totally unsuitable for any cob even if jumping is your aim. The horse's shoulders would be utterly inhibited in such a saddle.

best balance in a classical position. Why fight your own tack when you can select a saddle designed to help you move with your cob?

Bridle and bit

Regarding bridles and bits, keep it simple. First, start with a simple cavesson bridle and a simple snaffle bit. With regard to the bridle, make sure that the browband is long enough so that it doesn't make the headpiece pinch your cob's ears. Also, make sure too that it isn't too fine – a cob's head is not designed to wear a fine leather bridle such as might adorn a show pony! With regard to the noseband, make sure it is suitably thick – one of about 4cm (1½in or so) would be the most suitable width. When fitted, make sure it lies just two fingers' width under your cob's cheek bones and that, when done up, it isn't too tight around your cob's nose and jaws. Always make sure you can easily get a couple of fingers under the noseband.

For a cob who tends to put his tongue over the bit, a drop noseband could help. However, be sure not to fit it too low as this restricts the breathing. Also, don't fit it so tight that you restrict the movement of the jaw.

For a cob who doesn't respect a simple French link or any other double-jointed snaffle, then a vulcanite mullen-mouthed Pelham may be a better option. In intelligent hands it can be a fantastic remedial bit which allows you to be light on the reins and your cob to develop

right Here Wizard shows his snaffle bridle. This bridle is particularly suitable because of the appropriate width of the noseband. The fit of the throatlash is loose enough, but the browband could be longer. Wizard has a Baucher snaffle, a particularly useful bit.

far right Ketchup wearing her double bridle. The photo shows the fit of the curb chain and an appropriate lip strap.

self-carriage. The curb rein can be used gently to relax the cob's jaw by virtue of a reflex point that lies in your cob's curb/chin groove. All instructions for rein aids in this book work with a snaffle or a Pelham bridle. However, be sure not to be strong in your rein aids if using a Pelham, because over-strong rein aids with this bit can injure your cob's lower jaw.

Movement

Rhythm and activity are the key words when talking about movement. Cobs are usually very active creatures – at least when they are allowed to be. They tend to have very good, regular rhythmical gaits, possibly as a result of their 'four-square' conformation. Also as a result of their conformation, cobs tend to have rounded 'baroque' gaits, rather than the daisy-cutting gaits of a Thoroughbred. Some cobs, with certain breeding and/or a more upright shoulder, will have markedly accentuated knee action and perhaps a slightly jerkier movement.

In walk, a cob will usually swing well through the four-beat sequence, moving with some purpose. Although the stride length of a typical cob is not huge, it is not the length itself that is important, but the rhythm. Generally speaking, cobs don't have a huge overtrack in medium walk. They will tend to have an overtrack of less then a hoof width. This is because of the cob's typical conformation and movement. A cob is likely to make a higher, rounder movement with all four limbs than, for example, a Warmblood, and therefore the length of stride is shorter. A cob's quarters are also shorter that those of a Warmblood and this, coupled with more upright shoulders, means that all strides are made shorter. Of course longer-than-average quarters, more sloping shoulders and a shorter back, will allow a cob to overtrack more.

At trot, the cob's rhythm is usually great and the activity is second to none. However, take care that the cob's instinctive activity does not drive the trot rhythm too fast, as this can actually inhibit the action of the hind legs, contract the neck, spoil expression and destroy the moment of suspension which helps to create a well-cadenced stride. As with walk, the stride is round and the length can be described as short to medium.

Especially during the initial schooling period, canter is often a cob's weakest gait. A partly or poorly schooled cob's canter can sometimes

Here Helen with her delightful cob Mister Mints show a soft, round and 'uphill' canter.

be characterized by a slight flattening of the gait without expression, lacking in a moment of suspension and often really quite heavily on the forehand. This is often because a cob has powerful quarters that are more than able to push forward; the quarters are more often more powerful than he is able to manage. Often, in the early days, a cob can't balance the sheer power of his quarters and ends up weighting his bulky shoulders all the more. This results in a flat canter on the cob's shoulders, losing its rhythm and suspension. However, with correct schooling the canter can be improved markedly, even to the extent of becoming the best gait, light and expressive, with the hind legs clearly take the weight and the moment of suspension being clearly seen.

Generally speaking, the four-square nature of the cob helps contribute to movement that is straight and free in all gaits. However in some cases (for example, cobs bred from crosses with such breeds as Dales and Clydesdales) the movement can have a characteristic dishing. In dressage, the judge isn't going to look at the dishing; it is only potentially going to be an issue in the show ring. Of course, in a breed class in which it is a breed characteristic, it won't be taken into account. However, if you take your cob in a traditional show cob class, then the judge will place a cob with straight movement ahead of one with a dishing action, so long as the cob with straight movement is of the same or better overall quality and conformation.

CHAPTER TWO

The Rider's Qualities

What I am about to describe is not 'my' method, or a 'Cob's Can' method. It is a classical system that is taught by many classical trainers internationally. I was taught these methods by the instructor for whom I worked and there are others I know and respect who use and teach these techniques. There are also other books on the market that go into more detail about how to ride using these approaches.

It is my firm belief that the rider can make or break the relationship with and progress of any horse – cobs naturally included. It is down to the rider to optimize any situation. I am not trying to brow-beat the riding public but I do want to emphasize that, very often, what the horse is blamed for is actually the rider's fault. A rider's best quality is humility and the ability to put their hands up and say, 'OK, this time I was wrong, I shouldn't have done that.' Such riders are the ones who will make progress much quicker because they are generally more aware of their faults and more willing to correct them. A rider with an open and observant mind is more likely to notice an important fault creeping in and implement a strategy that will eliminate it.

In addition to this humility and thirst to correct every fault, the rider needs a few other basic tools; tools which will inform and provide stability. A correct classical position and alignment, achieved in relation to the individual's own conformation and capabilities, will allow for the correct absorption and influence of the horse's movement.

Before we discuss the classical or correct position let's think about our own individual situations. It is important to remember this while working towards an ideal. Rider conformation, experience, injury, physical condition and balance may inhibit us from achieving the ideal at any given time. As we work away on our riding and we develop our skills, we may be able to get closer to the ideal.

What I am saying is that there may be things at the moment that are stopping us from achieving these ideals, but that should not stop us from working towards them. Neither should they inhibit our desire to work our cobs using classical methods with the aim of attaining wonderful results.

The riders pictured in this book are at different points of experience and are at different points on the scale of achieving the ideal. They are all doing a fantastic job schooling their heavier mounts despite any limitations of experience, physical conditions or injury. The point is they are all progressing towards that ideal, their cobs are improving vastly and their riding is developing beautifully! They all have the ideal in their mind's eye but that is not inhibiting them from enjoying and progressing in their schooling of their cobs to the higher levels. You do not have to be perfect to start on the schooling journey; you just need the desire to improve towards it.

Helen is exhibiting a lovely 'classical' position. Her ears, shoulders, hips and heels are in vertical alignment. Her elbows are down by her side and her 'backline' shows a soft, gentle curve.

The default 'classical' position

This is the basic position which will provide stability for the rider, thereby offering the optimum position from which to absorb all the movements of the horse and from which to apply the most discreet and effective aids. It is also the healthiest position for both the rider and the horse, ensuring that neither is affected in a negative way that could cause injury. In fact, from the rider's perspective, this position is thought of by some as a healthy 'therapy' to prevent back injury since it aligns the back correctly and prevents damage to the muscles around the spine and the fluid-filled discs in between the vertebrae.

The key words when talking about the rider's classical position are 'vertical' and 'toned'. Vertical as in standing on the ground, with a straight vertical line from the ear, through the shoulder and the hip and down through the ankle bone – or heel if your conformation inhibits it being your ankle bone. (I believe it should be the ankle bone if at all possible, not the heel as is usually taught. Just think about it – if you are to be 'seated on a horse as when standing on the ground' then why would your heel rather than your ankle bone be under the centre of you body? Indeed, your heel is generally further back. If your heel rather than your ankle bone is under your seat, then there could be a tendency for you to roll back a little on your seat bones and onto the fleshy part of the buttocks and thus fall a little behind the movement. This is, of course an extreme situation, but it does highlight the slightly incorrect tendency of this seat.)

The pelvis

I believe the correct position depends entirely on the correct alignment of the pelvis. If the pelvis is in the correct position then it is much easier for the rider to align the back correctly and allow the leg to drop gracefully down in the form of a deep-set thigh and a well-placed lower leg. The pelvis is, in principle, the part of the rider's skeleton that comes into contact with the saddle and with the horse's back. I say 'in principle' because obviously around the pelvis you have the muscles of your upper legs and seat. However, when sitting in the saddle you should feel that your seat bones connect to the saddle through the thinner muscles at the base of your gluteals and at the top of your thighs. If you feel as though you are sitting solely on the thickest part of your bottom (your gluteals) then you are more than likely sitting with your pelvis tilted back.Therefore the pelvis must be aligned correctly.

In the classical position the pelvis must be upright and vertical. On the lowest plane of the pelvis lie two protruding edges known as the seat bones. When the pelvis is upright the seat bones effectively come into contact with the saddle. If the pelvis is in front of the vertical the pubic bone comes into contact with the saddle and forms the 'fork seat', which is not only uncomfortable for the rider but also inhibits the horse's forward movement and makes the rider 'bounce'. If the pelvis is behind the vertical this creates the 'chair seat' where often the buttocks take the weight of the rider and push on the back part of the saddle, which incidentally corresponds with the weakest part of the horse's back. It also creates an incorrect curve in the rider's back – which can strain it – and causes the ugly 'nodding head syndrome'. In

The classical seat is the basis for all riding and schooling. It can be, and should, be adapted for each situation as I have done here for the piaffe.

the cob it can create a hollow, dropping back or a tense, locked back. This seat is often described as the 'driving' seat, and indeed it is, but by pushing down on a weak part of the horse's back its main function is to drive the horse 'hollow'. (Fortunately, this is not the only way to drive with the seat, as will be discussed later when talking about absorption of the movement.)

Incorrect pelvic alignment can also affect the leg position. If the rider's pelvis falls in front of the vertical, then the rider's legs often (though not always) fall too far back, and if the rider's pelvis falls behind the vertical then the legs are often (though not always) pushed too far forward.

The back

Only with a correctly aligned pelvis can the rider's back and torso align correctly. With a correctly aligned pelvis, the shoulders should be positioned vertically above the pelvis. When the shoulders are positioned in this way a little 'tone' is added to the posture by thinking of lifting the diaphragm, toning the abdominals and allowing the shoulders to drop a little down and back. When I say tone, I mean tone and not tension. To explain the effect of toning a little more, when I talk about toning the abdominals I tend to think of someone poking me in my belly. What would your reaction be? Imagine it and think of your reaction. This reaction is that of toning the abdominal muscles. Toned muscles allow graceful movement; tense muscles restrict desirable movement and can only promote bounce.

With an incorrectly positioned back, the alignment of the spine will be impaired and injury could result. Generally, if the pelvis is in front of the vertical, so too will be the upper body and this is accompanied by a hyperflexion of the spine which fatigues the muscles and puts pressure on the fluid-filled discs. When the pelvis is behind the vertical then the back has no natural curve and is indeed flexed the wrong way. This too, causes fatigued muscles and pressure on the discs. I believe this to be one of the most dangerous positions for the rider and it does no favours to the horse.

The head and neck

The head needs to be vertically above the rider's torso. It should be straight and level and in general the rider's eyes should look where the horse and rider are going. Although it should not be loose or 'floppy', there should be no tension in the neck. Holding the chin in or jutting it out are both big mistakes – instead, a sense of easy mobilization and soft movement will help prevent stiffness in the head and neck. Ideally, the ears should be in line with the shoulders, hips and ankle bones, but I think that really depends upon the rider's conformation.

The legs

Again, if starting with an upright pelvis, positioned well forward on the twist of the saddle, the rider's legs will hang in a generally relatively vertical position close to the saddle and the horse. The knee, in a classical position, has a slight bend, and is by no means straight. The ankle bone is positioned directly under the hip and shoulder. When the foot is placed in the stirrup the heel is positioned slightly lower than the toe, though not forced down and generally, if the thigh is positioned well the toe is positioned pretty much under the knee. If the leg is positioned with a more forward-set thigh, then the rider will be viewed as having a seat without sufficient depth. In this type of seat the lower leg is pushed into an area of less sensitivity on the horse, reducing the effectiveness of the aids and thus impairing the rider's control. Also, this positioning often pushes the rider into a 'chair seat', balancing on the buttocks rather than the more effective seat bones. Alternatively, if the rider positions the thigh more vertically than necessary, then the lower leg is forced too far back into another area in which the leg becomes less effective, and the rider is compelled to assume a 'fork seat' and to balance on the knees rather than the seat bones.

The arms and hands

From the shoulders downwards, there should be no tension in the arms and hands. The shoulders need to be straight, not rounded and therefore the rider needs to think of closing the shoulder blades and bringing them back and down in order to bring the shoulders to the preferred position. The upper arms usually hang relaxed in a vertical position by the rider's upper body. If the shoulders are rounded then the upper arms will fall in front of the desired position. This will then have a negative effect on the contact between the hands and the horse's mouth as it will lose its elastic quality. The hands are held in front of the body; the rider should always think of the hands going forward and down to the horse's mouth rather than up and back to their own body. This will then help to maintain a desired straight line between the rider's elbows through the forearms and hands into the reins and down to the horse's mouth. Generally speaking, a position slightly in front and above the pommel of the saddle is about where you want your hands with a novice or fairly unschooled horse. The hands should be slightly higher for a more advanced cob with a higher head-carriage. The thumbs should be held on the highest plane, grasping the rein between the thumb and first finger. Wrists should not be stiff as this will have a negative affect on the connection between the horse's mouth and the rider's hand. Try not to be too obsessive about these positions; it could end up with you stiffening and making your hands rigid. These are just guidelines, and shouldn't be considered arbitrary. Your hand position should always relate to what you are asking your cob to do. Follow the guidelines in this book and you shouldn't go too far wrong.

Riding style in the show ring and hunting field

I think anything that you have read above in connection with position will work well in the show ring. However, for the hunting field or other cross-country riding, a position closer to that discussed in Chapter 5 in connection with jumping may be more appropriate. You will see riders maintaining a more 'defensive' position, as I describe it, across country – as well as the showing rings. Generally, the lower leg will be more forward than my ideal and the upper body will also be inclined a little more forward. I do think, however, that for the correct schooling of your cob and appropriate balance and absorption of the movement, the position that I have described should be worked towards. While the 'hunting seat' or defensive posture may be adequate at the lower level of schooling, it would be impossible to ride like this at the higher levels and it would also be less comfortable for your cob.

Absorbing movement – dynamic use of the default position

If you were to sit on your cob, and maintain what I have termed your default position, and not move at all when your cob moves, then unfortunately you would actually be hindering the movements that are projected through the cob's back and into the saddle. This would make things uncomfortable for both cob and rider and would eventually make the cob resistant and unwilling. In trot and canter such an attempt at total immobility on the rider's part would actually result in the rider bouncing involuntarily, threatening injury to the spines of both parties. What is necessary, therefore, is not enforced immobility on the rider's part, but very subtle harmonization with the cob's movement. This process starts, of course, from the default position, but then entails small, controlled movements of the rider's spine, hips and, to some extent, thighs. Although the rider can control these movements they are, to a large extent, dictated by the movements of the cob. Thus, in a sense, the rider needs both to anticipate and to 'follow' these movements. To a large extent, the former is a product of understanding equine movement at the different gaits and the latter is a product of 'feel' and rapport with the individual cob. When these factors combine successfully, so that the rider's movements mirror those of the cob, from an observer's point of view both will appear to be moving as one entity. If the rider fails in these endeavours, it is then that errors such as bouncing seat, nodding head, flapping legs and unsteady hands will become evident.

Now let's look at how harmony of movement is achieved at the individual gaits.

The walk

The walk is the cob's slowest gait and, as it doesn't have a moment of suspension, it is also the gait with the least upward thrust. Because of this it is the best gait in which to learn these controlled flexions of the back and the use of hips while riding. You can even practise these flexions before you get on your cob, by using a stool, or dining chair. Start off by ensuring an upright pelvis; feel that both seat bones are pointing straight down and not slanting at an angle either forwards or back. Make sure your shoulders are directly above your hips. Then the first set of movements you make will involve pushing your tummy forward by no more than a couple of centimetres (less than an inch) and then bringing it back to the default position. (Note that you should never move backwards from the default position with your pelvis as this is unhealthy for your spine and indeed flattens your back and moves against your cob.) Practise this for a while on the stool. In one whole walk stride, there are four beats; each of these beats dictates one movement of the back and hips. Forward-back-forward-back, that is one walk stride.

That movement aligns you with the forward movement of your cob's walk stride. Unfortunately that is not all we need to do to align to the cob's movement. Next time you ride your cob, ask him to walk on and then close your eyes for a couple of strides (obviously only if your cob is reliable!). Notice how one side of his back drops as the hind leg on that side steps forward. Try it yourself; put your hands on your hips. As you take a step with your left leg, your left hip lowers; as your left foot is put back on the ground your left hip is pushed up again (likewise with right leg!). So to make up for that movement of the cob's back you too must make a movement to align yourself and prevent hindrance. So, again, practise on a stool. As you push your stomach forward, think about pushing your left hip forward more than the right, then bring it back to straight, then flex again, but this time push your right hip more forward than the left.

These movements really help to align you not only to the forward crest of movement but also the lateral roll of the stride. Think about what these movements do to your body. As you push your left hip more forward, your left seat bone rises slightly and allows your cob's back on that side to rise; your left leg allows for the swing of the cob's barrel and allows the opposite leg to engage, and when your right hip is flexed more forward then your right seat bone rises, allowing room for the cob's back on that side, your right leg allows for the swing of the barrel and allows your left leg to engage. So as the left side dips, you need to allow your left seat bone to lower to enable it to maintain contact with your cob's back, and likewise for the right. Also, as his back rises on one side, allow his movement to raise the seat bone on that side slightly higher by flexing your back on that side a little more.

In summary, practise as follows:

1. From default classical position.

2. Flex spine forward with left hip more forward.

3. Flex back to default position.

4. Flex spine forward with right hip more forward.

5. Flex back to default position.

6. Flex spine forward with left hip more forward.

And so on and so forth.

I want to stress here that there is no overt swaying or thrusting of the seat from side to side, nor should you move any more that the cob dictates. Too much movement is a driving seat, and can push him into a more unbalanced way of going. Too little movement is akin to not doing anything at all; it becomes a hindrance for your cob when he is trying to move with this unyielding seat retarding every movement.

Sitting trot

Even though walk is four-time and trot is two-time, the movements for sitting trot are actually identical to those for walk, the only changes are the speed of the 'forward and back' flexions and the degree of these flexions. Because the trot has more thrust per stride, the rider's back needs to flex correspondingly, possibly with more of a pronounced advancing of each hip as the hind leg on that side has stepped under and is grounded. The best way to practise is to ask your cob to 'bounce' for about five or six strides, because if you practise too long, your muscles become fatigued and then you stiffen. If the bounce gets too fast, then it can become too difficult for you to co-ordinate your movements. Just stick to five or six strides at first; gradually you can extend this both by number of strides and strength of stride. Soon you will find that you can manage a full working or collected trot for a full circuit of the school, and beyond!

Rising trot

The movement of the rising trot need not be as strenuous as a lot of riding instructors would have you think. If you are in a sweat, then I suggest that you are doing too much! First, you need to angle your body very slightly (and the key is *very slightly*) forwards in front of the vertical. I recommend this because of a basic law of physics, because of the forward movement. You must take into account the forward momentum in the trot and because your position is constantly changing in relation to the horse, then allowances must be made for this. If you maintain a wholly upright position throughout, you will inevitably get left behind the movement. This happens because as you sit and are in a moment of 'status quo' the cob is still moving forward and, in order to rise again, you need to move your hips forward and often the shoulders get left behind. If this happens your movement then has to be huge and all the pressure generally falls to the back of the saddle area, the weakest part of the cob's back so, as well as being out of balance you are materially interfering with the cob's way of going.

However, with your body slightly angled forward from the hips the forward momentum is absorbed as a result of the hips swinging forward and back. The forward impetus propels your pelvis forward. How far

Janice showing ideal posture in the sit phase of rising trot.

Janice in the full and balanced rise phase of the rising trot. In the rise phase you should only go as far as the horse pushes you (generally to this balance point).

forward depends on the power generated beneath you, but it is generally sufficient for your posterior to just clear the saddle and for your hips to be pushed towards the pommel. On the next phase of movement your hips come back to the saddle on a similar plane, only reversed. So your pelvis and body as a whole may be more upright when at the full extent of the rise but, as your body comes back, it does so slightly in front of the vertical in preparation of taking the forward impetus of the next trot stride.

If you rise correctly, your hands will be able to stay low and still. Your eyes should stay forward, looking where you are going. All in all I like the thought of the cob's movement pushing your pelvis forward and back with the 1,2,1,2 beat of the trot stride. Don't think of being too much in front of the vertical, as a jumping type position is wrong! Your aim is simply not to be left behind the movement and that is all – if you are in front of the vertical to the extent that it is noticeable then you have probably gone far too far.

There are a couple of common faults to avoid when rising to the trot. Many riders will tend to rise too high (some by standing in the stirrups); others will tend to 'pump their pelvis' too much. Both will unbalance your cob. The amount your cob propels you forward relates directly to how much you take your pelvis forward and up in the rising trot. If you feel as though you are making an effort to rise to the trot, if you feel that you are landing heavily in the saddle, or if you can feel/hear a double bounce when you sit, the likelihood is that you are doing too much. Also, if you are tending to push your pelvis in front of the vertical line level with your knee you are pumping it forward too much.

Canter

I find the canter is the most wonderful gait of all to ride; it is often the gait in which the rider gets their first feelings of collection and lift and, *when the canter is correct*, it can be the easiest gait to ride. However, especially with cobs, it does take some schooling to get to that level. As mentioned earlier, with some cobs canter can be their poorest gait initially and yet, with schooling, it often ends up their best. Of course, this can only happen if you ride correctly.

Sitting properly to canter is all down to a combination of flexions of your spine and your ability to use your seat and abdominals to lift the stride so that is becomes more 'uphill'. So, first imagine a canter stride and its 1, 2, 3, beats. At the start of the stride your position is basically the default position except that your outside leg will be behind the girth and your inside leg will be kept more forward at the girth. On the next beat of the canter you will begin to flex the lower part of your back forwards to allow your pelvis to tilt forwards slightly and then, on the last beat of the canter stride, you will push your spine forward a little more. Of course this all happens so fast that the flexions really occur

In the moment of suspension use your abdominals to straighten your spine and use your thighs to 'pull' your cob up

Flex your spine forward with the 1... 2... 3... beats of the canter stride

Canter absorption.

in one movement as the stride progresses through the beats, rather than a 'flex and stop' then 'flex a little more then stop'. In the moment of suspension your spine straightens ready for the next three beats of the following stride. It is when the canter is on its third beat that your abdominals and seat need to do their work. I tend to think of my abdominals working at this point to bring my pelvis to upright again and thus help the cob to 'jump up' in the moment of suspension. You can also use your thighs and buttocks in a kind of 'hugging and sucking up' action at this point to help produce a more 'uphill' frame and stride. Remember, however, that it is the cob's back that needs to move your pelvis and not the other way round. The only action that you need to think of consciously is the use of your abdominals and thighs/buttocks; let your cob do the rest. It will all become easier as he gets more

below Three views of canter. Note that I am not rocking my shoulders forward and back or 'polishing' the saddle. The middle photo shows how I use my back during the canter stride by flexing my spine forward with the 1...2...3... beats of the stride.

balanced, but don't give up; it is this position that will be your key to riding a better canter. 'Rowing' with your shoulders and 'polishing the saddle' in the way that a lot of instructors advocate will only drive a horse – and especially a cob – more and more onto his forehand. He will become much heavier and out of control, ploughing onto your hands.

The rider's basic position is the main tool for progression; it is from a correct position that your cob will gain all of the support he needs. You can never expect self-carriage and ideal posture from him if you neglect your own responsibilities. Correct basic position, and the correct absorption of movement on the rider's part means hindering the cob as little as possible and allowing him to express himself without being restricted in any way.

CHAPTER THREE

The Basic Aids

While teaching riders with young or inexperienced horses I often find myself saying the same things: 'You must always start with the lightest aids practical…that is the only way you will end up with a light ride!' and I stick to this wholeheartedly. I have seen a few riders get on their mounts (not just cobs) and ask them to walk on by giving their poor horse a thump in the ribs; generally these horses have not been taught to move forward off light aids and by never giving them this opportunity, they never will.

Although transitions are like a young horse's ABC, they seem quite often 'left to chance' by riders and trainers – probably more so with the 'average' cob than with other types of equine. When I bought Ketchup, I used to resort to quite hard thumps to get her to move forwards. When she eventually moved forwards the rhythm was erratic and the forwardness was uncontrolled. She was so severely on her forehand that she was very heavy in my hands, and once we got her going it was so very hard to stop. She was 'numb' to the leg, ignorant of the hand, heavy and with uncontrollable forward movement. Fortunately, through re-education, Ketchup has become vastly lighter and more responsive.

Forward movement and upward transitions

Halt to walk

So, how do we start this process of education? Imagine you're aboard your cob stood in halt – make sure you are in your default position, without tension, as described in the previous chapter. Your rein contact at this point need to be fairly allowing, so as not to discourage the forward movement. Initially, the only part of your body that needs to move is your lower leg. I generally like to think of the region just above the ankle bone as being the area that applies the 'forwards' aid so, with that in mind, the action is a slight squeeze and release of your lower leg. Some riders also like to think of their lower leg nudging a little in a forward action (and I mean think, as observers should not be able to see this!). Generally, this should work, but cobs who are used to heavier, cruder aiding may not even notice it. In that case, I would do exactly the same but this time give a small flick with the schooling whip at the same time as my leg aid. I generally find that this works because most horses who have been broken-in in a traditional manner respect the whip and recognize it as a legitimate 'forwards' aid. However, very rarely in the breaking-in process are horses (and more often cobs, in my opinion) actually taught that legs can mean 'forwards'.

In a lot of cases I will re-educate a cob by actually taking a step back and teaching him what a leg aid means by asking a competent friend to use a lunge whip at the same time as I use my legs in very frequent transitions. Soon, the person with the lunge whip will be asked to take a step back and allow me to take a more dominant role. This is exactly how I teach youngsters to respond to the leg during my breaking-in process (which is often the stage nowadays omitted from other horses' education). I will then ride onto a 20m circle and aim to ride forwards from halt into walk, walk for up to ten strides then return to halt. (Halting is addressed under Downward Transitions, later this chapter.) I will repeat this, rewarding the cob when he moves into walk, and when he moves from light leg aids, I will really make a fuss of him. I will aim for about fifty transitions in all and suggest, if you can't achieve this, do as many as you possibly can. (While the youngster may not recognize 'forward' leg aids at this

In an upward transition, or as a reminder to move forwards, use both legs together in an inward and forward roll.

Using the forward aids.

stage, he will respond reasonably well to the 'steering' aids on a circle
if he has become accustomed to working on a circle on the lunge.)

The moment there is movement from the halt into walk, I allow the
cob to move my seat as described in the previous chapter, and maintain
forward impetus by applying light leg aids with the swing of the cob's
belly, left leg as the belly swings from the left side to the right (when the
left shoulder moves back) and then the right leg as the belly swings
from the right to the left (when the right shoulder moves back.) If the
cob starts to slow down in walk I will not increase the strength of
the leg aids but again give a flick with the schooling whip just behind
the leg. A lot of riders seem to think that giving a horse a flick with the
schooling whip is being cruel, but in my opinion it is far better for his
welfare than resorting to numbing thuds on his side that will inevitably
cause bruising, or trying to push him along with a heavy 'shoving' seat
that will put pressure on his tender back.

Walk to trot

The process of moving from walk to trot is very much the same. The rider
prepares by checking position and checking the length of reins. The
unilateral use of the legs in walk is then altered to a closing of both legs
with a 'squeeze and release' action. If the walk has been active, this is
usually enough to move the cob from walk up to trot. If this doesn't work,
follow the process of repeating the same level of leg aids, reinforced with
a flick of the schooling whip, until the desired movement is achieved.
Then remember to move forward with your cob in the way described
in the previous chapter for rising trot. Again, if there is a real lack of
understanding on the cob's part, you can enlist the help of a competent
friend with a lunge whip. This exercise is only ever needed a few times
before the cob really does understand. However, it is well worth your
while taking this step back if you are at all unsure whether your cob un-
derstands your 'forwards' aids. I am sure that this preparatory work is the
key to a forward-going light ride that both you and your cob will enjoy.

Once the trot is established, I would again suggest moving onto a
large circle and riding a series of transitions (see next section) with
about ten strides between each, rewarding the cob whenever he responds well and the moment he moves forward off the light leg aids.

I must emphasize at this point the importance of rewarding your mount. If going from halt to walk, the moment your cob moves into walk, let him know that this is what you want. Tell him by using a kind tone and giving him a good scratch in front of the saddle on the side of his neck. Do the same when moving from walk to trot – let him know when he has done what was required and you will find that he will learn even quicker as he will become more willing to have a go. When he knows exactly what you want, he will give it to you; by praising him in this way you will find that he will acquire a thirst for praise, and this means that he will constantly be thinking about what you are asking for and how to give it…all so he can have a scratch and a pat and a few kind words. (This is the biggest key to training.)

Trot to canter

Trot to canter is probably the hardest upward transition to make because initially it is generally as difficult for the average cob to maintain an even trot rhythm before the transition as it is for the average rider to maintain their position during the transition. What generally happens is that the cob runs into a faster trot as the rider asks for the canter, the rider then feels that the cob is 'unwilling' to canter and gives the aids more strongly. The cob then loses balance before the transition and when it is finally achieved the result is a fast, flat and uncontrollably heavy canter.

I think it is often far better to keep the canter out and about in the open until you have built up enough activity to pop up into canter from walk. Either way, the aiding is exactly the same; in walk the rider maintains the position as described earlier, and from trot the rider generally goes into sitting trot and maintains that position without the trot rhythm faltering. The rider's aid for the canter is to position the outside leg back behind the girth. This has to happen from the hip and not just from the knee. This leg is what I often call the indicator, as it tells the cob which leg to strike off from. However, it does nothing more than brush the cob's coat. The rider's inside leg is kept forward at the girth (as a result of the inside hip being placed forward and the outside hip being back) and is the more dominant leg. It is used in a forward squeeze and release, with a feeling of lifting the cob's belly. This should be enough to instigate the first canter strike-off, but in reality it often isn't. The way to remedy this is to use exactly the same exercise as mentioned earlier with your trusted friend and the lunge whip and to ride 'fifty canter transitions' – well, I mean lots!. Ride a 20m circle, and ask for a canter transition helped by your companion; aim to ride four or five strides of canter before returning to trot. Re-establish the trot before you aim for your next canter transition and gradually ask your companion to do less and move away. (Again, remember to reward your cob when he canters, and the moment he canters from a light leg aid really make a fuss of him.)

Downward transitions

If upward transitions form the 'A' part of the ABC, then downward transitions constitute the 'B' (and turning, of course, is the 'C'). Although response to the 'forward' aids is fundamentally important, it is just as important for the horse to respond readily and correctly to the downward aids. A cob with no 'brakes' is as dangerous as a car with its brakes tampered with! Imagine trotting willy-nilly along a road heading towards a busy crossroads, or being carted at canter towards a barbed-wire fence.

I'm sure most cob owners have experienced a ton weight in their hands as they hauled their mount to a halt. When Ketchup first came to me that is exactly how she was. She was only 3 years old and had already been schooled in the 'traditional' manner. To bring her from walk to halt, a small movement from my fingers wasn't enough. She had been 'taught' that if the rider 'felt' her mouth, she had to push onto the contact. This is only a natural reaction – we all know that when we try to push a horse who is standing on our toe, he pushes back with just as much force – this reaction is the exact same re-action, a reaction to the pressure exerted on the mouth. So not only did Ketchup need indiscreet if not heavy leg aids to get her to move forward, she also needed her rider to be an accom-plished weight trainer to have the strength to bring her to halt! It would have been much easier to have had a newly backed youngster without these negative training features.

All downward transitions are initiated in essentially the same way. They are a combined action of your seat muscles (upper thighs and buttocks) and your 'centre' muscles in your abdomen. The reactions to 'downward' aids described

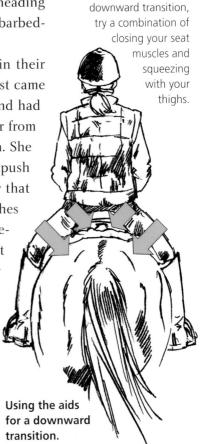

When riding a downward transition, try a combination of closing your seat muscles and squeezing with your thighs.

Using the aids for a downward transition.

49

below work (albeit in hesitant fashion) from the moment you first back a baby, on their very first ride.

From walk

Let's start with a walk to halt transition. As your cob walks along it is just a case of feeling as though you are firming up your buttocks, closing your upper thigh muscles, and feeling that you 'connected with your centre' – that is to say a slight toning of your lower abdominal muscles. At the same time as these aids, it is often beneficial to have a feeling of growing tall through your torso. Some cobs need more thigh muscle aids than others. Some need more buttock aids. So it really is a question of getting to know which is your cob's preferred aiding. The key however is not to put any more tension through the reins. Remember, if you put pressure down through the reins, then all you will get back from your cob is pressure doubled.

From trot

Downward transitions from trot to walk can be divided into two types, one from a rising trot and the other from an established sitting trot. If you are in an established sitting trot the procedure is exactly the same as outlined above. However, if you are rising, one of the most unbalancing things you can do is make the downward transition through a few strides of sitting trot. This is because the cob suddenly feels a change in your balance and is often going a little more onward than he would be if you had been sitting to the trot initially. This creates more bounce in the stride that often isn't absorbed adequately, causing bounce and tension in the rider and an inevitable pull on the reins. All this is a recipe for a disastrous downward transition: the bounce in the stride will be amplified, the cob will get heavier in the mouth, and often he will 'run away' from the pressure, getting faster and stronger rather than slower. So, if you are in rising trot, all you have to do is simply slow down the frequency of your rising and sitting. On each of the sitting phases you need to have a feeling of closing your seat muscles, and your 'centre' muscles. You will find that your cob tries to balance his strides with you and that he moves into a walk without hollowing, pulling or getting stronger.

Wizard responding to Anne's slowing aid in rising trot. You can see the flexion in his joints as he takes the weight onto his hocks.

For a trot to halt transition, which is usually carried out from an established sitting trot, all you have to do is to use the same aids as above but with a little extra strength and duration. Don't worry – your cob will let you know how strong you need to be with these invisible aids and I think you'll be surprised at how little you will eventually have to do.

From canter

Downward transitions from canter are exactly the same in principle: vary the strength as required, a soft squeeze of the seat muscles for a transition to trot, a stronger squeeze for a transition to walk, and an even stronger squeeze to go to halt. The key, however, for your cob continuing to go forwards in these downward transitions, is to be prepared to synchronize your movements with the movements made in the new gait. Be ready to move with the trot, or the walk, or to stay neutral in the stationary halt.

Turning

Have you ever felt the horse you were riding drift out through his outside shoulder? Have you ever used more inside rein to turn your mount only to find that this makes him drift out even more? Or have you ever turned your shoulders into the direction of the turn only to find that this pushes the horse out towards the corner of the school rather than turning across it? Well, these are often what are experienced by many cob owners and they are as a result of various misconceptions about how a horse turns and the aids for turning.

The weight aids are essentially a product of the position of the pelvis and the various flexions of the rider's lower back. Basically a weight aid occurs as the rider, in flexing the spine forward, pushes the bony part

Anne showing the essential ingredients for a turning aid. Her inside hip is placed forward, she is looking into the direction of the turn and her outside hand is supporting without being restrictive.

The outer view of the turning aids. Anne's outside leg is placed back, not from the knee but from the hip. A view not always appreciated by riders and instructors.

of their hip a little more forward on one side than the other. This has an effect on the weight distribution on the seat bones which are in close contact with the saddle and therefore influence the horse's back. By pushing the bony part of your hip a little more forward or, as many teachers say, 'advancing the hip' you are pushing more weight into the seat bone. When this happens I like to use the analogy of a waiter with a heavy tray. As the weight distribution of the objects on the tray changes then the waiter needs to move 'under' the direction of the weight. And in this vein your horse will do the same; he will feel your weight a little more into the particular seat bone and will move into its direction to 'catch up' with it. If you push the bony part of your hip a little more forward on the left, then the horse will move to the left, and the same happens to the right.

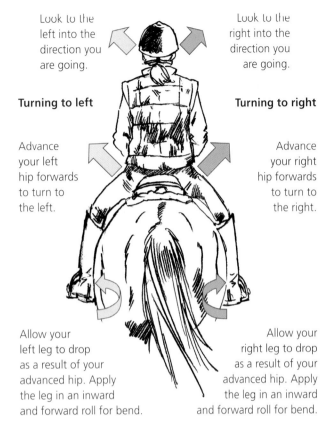

Look to the left into the direction you are going.

Look to the right into the direction you are going.

Turning to left

Turning to right

Advance your left hip forwards to turn to the left.

Advance your right hip forwards to turn to the right.

Allow your left leg to drop as a result of your advanced hip. Apply the leg in an inward and forward roll for bend.

Allow your right leg to drop as a result of your advanced hip. Apply the leg in an inward and forward roll for bend.

Using the turning aids.

Often, instructors will ask the rider to turn their shoulders to the inside into the direction of the turn. When the rider does this on my horses the horse merely follows the weight of the rider and instead of turning, ends up pushing with their shoulders to the outside and drifting more to the outside rather than following the correct line of the circle or turn. The reason why this happens is all down to the weight distribution of the rider in the saddle. For example, if you ask your cob to turn to the left using this technique, you will be required to turn your shoulders to the left. This inadvertently pushes your left hip and seat bone back while advancing the right hip and weighting the right seat bone. So to the cob, the instruction is to go right, not left! You can see how easily confusion can creep in.

If we go back to how we absorb our cob's movement in walk or sitting trot, you will remember that we already advance our hips alternately as his back rises and falls unilaterally. So in this situation if, for example, we were to turn to the right, every time we advance our hip on the right-hand side we would advance it just a little bit more each time; this would be just enough to initiate a turn in that direction. More flexion is required for a smaller turn and of course each cob is different. An exercise that I find valuable when people come to ride Ketchup, is that I ask the riders to hold the reins at the buckle, ask her to walk and then just experiment with advancing one hip more than the other when absorbing the movement of her back. This is an exercise that I would recommend to anyone unsure of the method as, when it is experienced in such a way, it is not only illuminating but also magical for both cob and rider to experience. Both faces have expressions of gratitude – the cob thinks, 'Oh thank goodness, now they've learnt to ride!' while the rider thinks, 'How can I have gone so long without knowing this!'

In rising trot, however, things happen slightly differently. As your hips move forward in the rising phase of the stride it is at this moment that you would push the hip on the side of the turn a little more forward. So, in a left turn, push your left hip a little more forward as you rise while, in a right turn right, push your right hip a little more forward during the rise.

In canter the nature of the stride makes it fairly easy to advance your inside hip because the canter has a lateral bias owing to its leading leg. Therefore if you are in canter to the right, your right hip is often in advance naturally. Quite often it is simply a case of stretching a little taller in your waist and ribcage into the direction of the turn, coupled with the naturally advance hip.

All of these points, once mastered, are much easier for the rider to co-ordinate than to 'pull on this rein, kick with that leg and turn your shoulder there' – and of course it is much kinder for your mount than pulling heavily on the reins.

....

CHAPTER FOUR

Basic Novice Schooling

At the basic level of schooling the priorities are the foundations on which all future schooling depends. It is at this stage that your cob will become established in being a forward-going, sensitive ride; he will become light in hand and sensitive to your aids for downward transitions, he will learn to accept the contact of the bit and of course will learn how to be a rhythmical, supple and willing ride, all of which need to be established before thought of advancement can occur.

Fundamental aims

Some of the exercises outlined in this chapter will work on several of these early foundations or stepping stones; many are interdependent and develop several qualities simultaneously, but as your cob's trainer you will have to have the following elements in your mind as you school at home: responsiveness to aids for upward transitions/forwardness, responsiveness to aids for downward transitions, correct rhythm, correct bend and correct contact. The following are short descriptions of each and why they are so important in schooling your cob.

Responsiveness to upward aids / 'forwardness'

Any horse is said to be correctly 'forward', or 'in front of the leg' when he responds correctly to your forward-driving leg aids. That is, when you close your legs he responds by moving forwards either into a faster gait (for example from trot to canter) or by lengthening within the gait (for example from collected trot to medium trot). For your cob to be properly 'forward' he should also respect that when you put your legs on for forward movement, he shouldn't just run and push weight into your hands. When I talk about 'forwardness' I am always reminded of many top trainers saying 'forwardness is not speed', but how many trainers remember that when they are teaching? True forwardness is developed when your cob moves off your leg calmly, without hesitation but with balance. It is as a result of what his hind legs are doing. In correct 'forward' movement, each hind leg not only swings forward under the cob's body mass but, as it does so, it balances more weight into the hindquarters. Thus, when your cob is suitably forward, gone will be any semblance of a lazy slob, heavy in your hands, and in his place you'll find him transformed into an eager, enthusiastic fun ride who moves with surprising ease and agility.

Wizard looking 'forward' and responsive while engaging his hind legs well.

Responsiveness to downward aids

When your cob feels your seat aids close to bring about a downward transition, whether from one gait to another or within the gait (for example from medium canter to a more collected canter) and responds immediately without ignoring your aids or pushing onto your hands, then he is correctly responsive to your downward aids. This is an important stepping stone because without this responsiveness you will not have the ability to use a correct half-halt to rebalance your cob onto his hocks. With training, your cob should become more responsive to any such aids and this brings about an increased degree of manoeuvrability and really does help you get your cob off his forehand. Without this ability to 'change gear' whilst retaining a forward impulse in your cob with these aids, you are likely to resort to heavier methods using the reins, pulling him in his mouth with an inevitable loss of balance.

At an extreme level, the ability to apply correct half-halts and to get a correct response to downward aids can helps you to steady a 'rushing tank' and turn him into a rhythmical, steadily impulsive ride.

Correct rhythm

A cob who is suitably 'forward' and responsive to downward aids will usually also be moving in a correct rhythm, and a correct rhythm will help turn him into a beautiful, graceful gymnast. Rhythm is regularity of footfall and good rhythm requires that the footfalls are in the correct

Nicola riding Lucky in a rhythmical working trot. A good rhythm allows the stride to lengthen.

order and that the intervals are at a suitable distance apart for that horse in that gait. This is the 'speed' of that rhythm or the 'tempo'. Generally, a good rhythm and tempo are slower that we might think. If these qualities are too fast, they will often be associated with a horse 'running' to some extent on his forehand. When a horse is correctly 'forward' but in a more manageable rhythm then he will tend to put more of his weight onto his haunches; it will make him more manoeuvrable and much more controllable. When your cob is in a suitable rhythm with enough forwardness then his stride will be less restricted; because he has more weight on his haunches he will be able to use his hind leg joints more beneficially and to lengthen his stride correctly when so required.

A good rhythm also makes it much easier for the rider to synchronize their movements with those of their mount and makes it much easier to apply the aids invisibly.

I believe it is when you have achieved the three stepping stones of responsiveness to upward and downward aids and correct rhythm that you will begin to achieve true expression in your cob. By making sure he moves forward off your leg, and slows down from your seat (without contracting his neck in the way that is often seen with a taut rein) and, of course, by developing a 'tick-tock' rhythm, then you can sit your cob on his hocks, liberate his shoulders and allow him to really stride out and begin to develop cadence. (People can use 'cadence' to mean rather different things. My definition of cadence is when a horse has a fully developed regular rhythm and a certain freedom of movement, especially through liberated, light shoulders. He has sufficient energy within his stride so that he is not earthbound; he has enough energy to 'bound' over the ground. A cob with cadence has a higher stride than a cob without cadence. Cadence is the result of combining energy with engagement, rhythm and a developed contact which is connected to the hind legs.)

Correct bend

Correct bend makes any horse much suppler, straighter and softer. The suppleness means that he can bend easily in both directions. Your cob should be able to bend easily in both directions without any resistance or stiffness. The straightness comes as a result of correct and even

bending in both directions. Think about it like ironing his body out. Straightness doesn't only mean that your cob should gradually learn to move on straight lines without incorrect alignment, but also that he has the same ability to bend in both directions again without incorrect alignment. The softness occurs when the bend has been used to make your cob more malleable, so that he allows you to place him into any given bend without stress or force.

Two images of good bend for their level of training. Ketchup on the left shows more advanced lateral bend.

Correct contact

Correct contact is a result of forwardness, rhythm and bend – for example, if a horse is made straight by correct attention to equal lateral bend, this quality allows the energy produced by the hind legs to travel straight through his back and neck into a correct contact. Because of the symbiotic relationship of these different qualities, correct contact further enhances the other positive features of your cob's way of going.

For your cob to have a correct contact, he needs to be soft in the mouth, rounded in outline and always (unless he is being worked long and low – see later this chapter) with the axis/atlas joint in the poll as the highest point skeletally. Having said this, this can be difficult to ascertain with the more cresty type of cob as the crest can often make

Ketchup forward to the contact.

it look as though the third cervical vertebra is the highest. What I would say is that you need to look at whether the face of your cob is at or in front of the vertical rather than behind the vertical and whether he is soft and light in your hand. It is my opinion that your cob's face should never come behind the vertical. If it is at the vertical or just in front then all should be well.

For your cob to have a good contact he should be light in hand, with good flexion of the jaw and the poll. The muscles in the back and neck should be soft and in no way tense. Tense muscles mean a hard contact, a tense mind and the damaging of delicate tissues. The correct contact means that the energy produced by the hind legs is allowed to travel through your cob's back and neck. A correct contact thus has a positive effect on all of the other aspects of schooling mentioned above. Your cob becomes more responsive to both upward and downward aids, he becomes more manoeuvrable, his rhythm will improve no end and his suppleness and expression will improve greatly.

Modern training methods – a word of warning

There are some points at which the training methodology I follow diverges drastically from that followed by most current dressage competitors and trainers. Generally, most conventional dressage trainers follow a similar methodology whatever the size, make or shape of horse. Unfortunately, the methods they follow were initially designed for a very different kind of horse from the cobs that are the subject of this book. The training methods used in modern competitive dressage stables were developed for large, heavy horses of the old Warmblood type (essentially, carriage horses with just a small admixture – if any – of Thoroughbred-type blood). These horses were very often rather long in body shape, flatter in the croup and often rather less intelligent than our average cob. The methods developed from training such horses are more often than not, forwards, forwards, forwards. Riding in this way generally puts cobs much more onto the forehand and onto your hands (anyone who has ever ridden a cob in this way will know just how uncomfortable it is for the rider – never mind how uncomfortable it might be for the cob!). This is then counteracted by pulling more on the reins and pushing more with the legs in order to 'engage', but this only exacerbates the situation. Under such instructors we are made to have our cobs tracking up and even overtracking in collected movements, in a mistaken belief that this automatically means the cob is 'active' and taking weight behind. It seldom means, however, that the cob is actually putting more weight onto his haunches. In this stride pattern, the cob is then so forward and the hind legs are forced so far under his body that any spring and flexion that might produce cadence and expression are forced out of the joint system. This also flattens the stride, introduces more speed and the cob's centre of gravity is therefore lowered and moved forward, onto the forehand.

I have even seen trainers send cobs long and low, deep and round or even use rollkur for very long periods – which is a huge mistake owing to the conformation of most cobs' hindquarters. By putting a cob so low in front, and by the fact that a cob will most generally be well sloped behind, this will create too much tension in his back – especially if it is coupled with the modern tendency to go so forward as mentioned. Instead of using these methods, I tend to think of engaging the quarters by introducing more flexion into the hind leg joint system, I therefore follow the more classical French method of engaging the haunches by bending the joint system rather than by 'chasing' the hind legs more forward under the body, which introduces the problems mentioned above.

Making your cob softer and lighter

I suggest that you don't commence the work in this section until your cob will move forward off light aids and slow down with light aids as described in the 'upward aids' and 'downward aids' sections of the previous chapter. Continue with exercises described there until your cob is responsive, and then begin to use them in your warm-ups in preparation for the exercises that follow below.

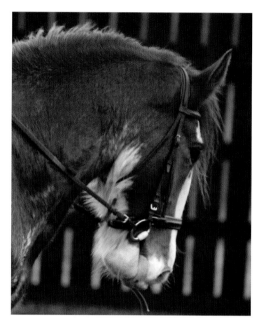

Any horse can soften in his mouth and poll to be ridden towards a more classically correct outline. Here Victor is doing a cracking job.

Flexions at halt

The first thing I will discuss here is a basic flexion of the cob's mouth that brings about an early softness in outline and begins to bring about lightness in his way of going. Generally I will start such flexions in halt. I will shorten my reins until a lot of the slack is taken out but without putting any extra weight onto the cob's mouth. Once the reins are the optimum length I will start squeezing on the reins, alternating between the two. I will squeeze two or three times on the left rein, then two or three times on the right. The reaction I am looking for at this early stage is for the cob to mobilize his mouth, soften his contact to the bit

and to round and curve his neck. This may take one or two squeezes or it may take much longer, as long as a minute or so. The key is to persevere! The moment your cob gives you the desired reaction really praise him, give him the reins, tell him 'well done!' and give him a good stroke or scratch. I would almost guarantee that if you have praised him well, then next time you ask he'll give it to you so much quicker.

Once your cob is accustomed to these aids and knows what is required of him, you will need to begin to release the reins slightly instead of giving the praise described above. You will also require him to flex his jaw and round his neck for longer periods, so once he is accustomed to these aids and responds to them diligently, rather than rewarding instantly you will require him to hold his position for longer. And to do this you must, once he has responded, release the reins by opening your fingers slightly so that no vibration is felt at all. This cessation of aids can be viewed as a mini reward and the fingers only need to close slightly around the reins and resume vibrations when he lifts his head again or puts weight onto the reins. Your cob will soon get the idea and maintain a steadier head position.

above left Here I am showing Sarah how to flex and soften Smokey to ask him to carry himself in a rounder way.

above right Here Smokey responds exactly as I wanted.

Flexions into walk and trot

When your cob will consistently give you this flexion when asked for it at the halt, it is time to ask for it during a transition to the walk. In halt, ask for the flexion. When he gives you the flexion, close your legs as described in Chapter 3 for a transition to walk. Maintain the

Sarah achieves the softness in movement.

alternating squeeze of the fingers so that you keep saying to your cob 'stay soft please' and you may well get your first soft, rounded transition to the walk. If this doesn't work and your cob pushes his head up and loses the lightness in his mouth then you need to halt him as soon as possible and repeat the procedure. The moment you get the soft and round transition up to the walk, give praise that will reinforce the message that he has done as you wanted and has pleased you.

Once your cob is maintaining this softness in the walk, supported by your all-important release of the reins when all is well and flexing of the reins when needed, then, using the same aids in the fingers, you can ask for your transition into the trot. Again, the moment you lose the softness, return to halt and start again. Don't try to 'recover' the situation; it is far better to make a new attempt by starting afresh. (The same can be said of the later transitions to canter – however I would suggest waiting until your cob has developed enough collection to pop into the canter from a soft, rhythmical walk.)

One thing that I will emphasize here is that perseverance pays. The more consistent you are at this stage of the schooling routines, the more consistent your cob will be in giving you what you want – and remember, the more praise you give in such situations, the more likely he will be to give you what you want at anytime thereafter. Remember not to get stronger with your fingers if your cob doesn't respond immediately. If you get stronger, your cob will get heavier and that is the last thing we want – you will never win a battle of strength against a cob! Stay soft and be patient.

Transitions, transitions, transitions…

The pictures below show what can be achieved by riding transitions. Look at the differences between them: one is taken before the transitions exercise and the other after.

Once your cob is capable of moving forward off light leg aids, is responding to the aids for upward and downward transitions as described in Chapter 3, and is capable of maintaining softness as described above, then I recommend beginning to develop rhythm, cadence, expression and bend using repeated transitions on a 20m circle between the medium walk and the working trot. Bring your cob onto a 20m circle in walk, maintaining a soft mouth and a correctly arched neck. Ask for a little bend to the inside by increasing the pressure of the inside leg with the swing of the belly, and ask for the nose to come a little to the inside by raising your inside hand by a couple of centimetres (about an inch) and flexing softly to that side. Pick a point on the circle where you will make your upward transition to the trot; each time you get to this point is where you pick up the trot. Also decide where you will make the transition to walk. For example, I tend to use A as the position in the school to do my downward transition from trot to walk. I would then ride a quarter of a circle in walk before moving the cob back up

below left
Before: Nice trot . . .

below right
After: Fab trot . . .

to the trot when touching the outside track a little after either K or F, depending on the direction of travel.

At this stage I use this repetitive sequence to build some anticipation in my mount; an anticipation that I use to my advantage. The key here is to remember all that we have discussed so far. What you should begin to feel is a 'tick-tock' rhythm and a certain responsiveness that hasn't been felt before, as though your cob is reading your mind. Remember to do this work on both reins. The key is not to get heavier in any of your aids throughout this exercise; if anything seek to make your aids lighter and lighter.

Once your cob is settled in this exercise you can vary the positioning both of your transitions within the circle and of the circle itself. If at any time your cob starts to feel lazy, heavy or fast, then go back a step to the earlier exercises on basic transitions just to confirm your requirements. This exercise can be seen as the culmination of what has been done so far, in that you need to read your mount and respond appropriately using the techniques previously described. For example, the moment your cob speeds up the rhythm and tempo beyond what is comfortable, then make a downward transition to walk before re-establishing your trot rhythm. If your cob pushes onto your hands or brings his head higher than you want, make a downward transition and reconfirm the flexion and softness described earlier. This exercise really teaches you to read your cob and respond to his requirements.

Wizard enjoying transition exercises to really engage his hind legs and develop spring, and length of stride.

Once your cob is moving forward off light leg aids you can really begin to build that 'tick-tock' rhythm mentioned earlier. I really use the transitions to my advantage here. If there is any hint that the speed of the rhythm is getting too quick, then make a transition down to walk. Re-establish softness in the walk and repeat the transition to trot. In this transition be very mindful of the rhythm that you want and actively use your rise in the rising trot to dictate that rhythm. All of this needs to happen with a light contact so that there is nothing to inhibit your cob's expression and so that he doesn't feel restricted in his neck and begin to tense away from the contact. Likewise, if your cob gets heavy in your hands make a transition to walk or even halt, soften him and then make your upward transition again. If you are consistent in these respects, then your cob will soon realize that non-compliance will not get him anywhere and he will deliver a soft and rhythmical performance.

Schooling exercises

Now I will discuss elements of schooling which can be introduced once the transitions exercise is being accomplished without stress to you or your cob. These exercises are great for introducing a little more bend, making your cob a little more supple and soft in his outline and they will, of course, improve his rhythm no end. It is interesting to note that, at any point in your cob's training, once such milestones are achieved, the effects are far more far-reaching than one often thinks. For example, once you can introduce more bend, your cob's outline, rhythm, forwardness and engagement will improve vastly without actually working on these areas at all. And this concept carries on into more advanced schooling areas.

Lucky showing the benefits of the different school movements. Here, circling to the right, with nice bend.

In-hand work

Quite often, cobs can feel quite stiff and rigid in their bodies. Until Ketchup was able to bend correctly she would very often use her shoulders to her own advantage. Cobs who are so rigid can often bulldoze their way through anything and Ketchup was no exception. I remember her first dressage competition as a 4-year-old. She still wasn't too established in a controlled bend, and the stress of being at a competition meant that anything that she knew at home was a foreign language in the warm-up arena! Her shoulders were like snakes; one moment we were in the arena, the next she would bulldoze her way round the corner and over the dressage boards. Needless to say elimination followed. Does any of this sound familiar? A friend's cob, Sam, was so rigid that

Ideal postion for in-hand work.

he couldn't use his shoulders or even his body to his own advantage. He was so stiff through his ribcage that riding him in our 20 x 40m outdoor school was like manoeuvring an unyielding railway sleeper round a tiny garden shed! He just couldn't bend – though I think poor Sam was even more rigid in his mind than his body; he just didn't think it was possible! What I did to Sam is what I did with Ketchup a few years earlier, and it is what I have done with many horses, cobs and ponies with great success.

It is a method managed on foot rather than ridden. I will describe it here as if you were on the left rein but of course it must be done equally on both reins. Standing to the nearside of your bridled cob, level with or just behind his shoulder, you need to hold the left rein very close to the bit, close enough so that you can feel the bit at any time. Your right hand holds the right rein further back as it crosses your cob's back near the withers (see picture). While your cob is standing still you need to vibrate the rein in exactly the same way as when ridden to soften his mouth. When your cob softens, open your left hand slightly so that, with the vibrations of that hand, you are actually asking your cob to look a little to the inside. When he does so and maintains a soft outline, stop and praise him. Remember how praise works wonders! Once you are able to ask for this on both reins and achieve success every time, then it is time to make a move and begin to extend this exercise into walk.

So, ask your cob to round up, and look a little to the inside and once he has positioned himself in this way, ask him to walk on. Generally, if he has been well handled and is accustomed to the voice aids, your cob will walk on from your voice and a cluck of the tongue. If these aids don't work, you may need to carry a schooling whip in your right hand to just 'touch' your cob to initiate his transition into walk, or to have a helper on the ground using a lunge whip. In the walk you will need to walk alongside your cob with your body facing him, so you will be side-stepping (walking sideways but with your body fully facing towards your cob) to keep up. All the while you will need to vibrate the left rein a little to bring his nose a little to the inside (left) while he maintains a soft outline in his neck without pushing any weight onto your hands. You will need to be very aware of what his body is doing behind his neck, as when any horse bends, he must appear to do so equally all the way down his spine from his poll to his tail. So, with the left flexion in his neck, you will need to observe whether your cob pushes out with his right shoulder, producing too much 'neck bend', or whether he pushes too much weight onto his left shoulder and tries to fall in or make the circle smaller. If he falters in either of these ways, return via walk and correct it in halt. If he pushes his shoulders to the outside, your inside hand needs to do less and the outside rein, held in your right hand, needs to be a little more dominant and will have to act the moment he tries to push weight onto the outside shoulder. So, the moment you feel this happening, think inside rein 'stop and let go', steps slow down and outside rein vibrates to correct too much neck bend. If your cob pushes too much weight towards you, onto his left shoulder, then start in halt to have a feeling of pushing his shoulders over slightly towards the right, with your right hand positioned either on the shoulder or just behind it where the girth would go if he were saddled. Always have a feeling of 'pushing' the circle a bit bigger if this is the problem with your cob.

This in-hand bending exercise can be done a little on straight lines but I would mainly do it on circles of varying sizes down to about 10–8m in walk. Of course, changes of rein will inevitably mean halting your cob in order for you to change the side on which you are standing. Such changes of rein must be frequent to make sure your cob is being 'ironed out' correctly and adequately on both reins. This exercise is great as part of your daily warm-up programme.

Once this can be achieved you can begin to ask for a little more bend when you ride your cob and you can also introduce different movements into your schooling repertoire that really work on bend and suppleness. Some movements, such as circles, just work on bend and suppleness in one direction at a time. Other movements, by design, look for suppleness in changes of bend and vary in difficulty, such as half-circles returning to the track with a change of rein (tear drop shapes), 3 and 5m loops in from the track and of course, serpentines.

Circles

In circles, of course, the shape must be exactly round. You often see horse and rider combinations produce squares with the corners rounded off and yet it needn't be like that. To ride a circle correctly you need to remember your weight aids, so you need to advance your inside hip a little and deepen your inside leg. Your inside leg needs to stay forward at the girth as it asks for a little bend through the ribcage. Your inside rein flexes your cob to the inside so you can just see the corner of his eye. Your outside rein supports the flexion indicated by your inside rein and, along with your weight aids, prevents your cob's shoulders from falling out. With this in mind I always say, 'Ride out to your circle'. By this I don't mean push him out with your inside leg, what I mean is project your body in that way. This pushes the inside hip a little more forward and often helps the rider to support their mount's outside shoulder. Keep looking a few steps in front of where you are riding and all should be well. Remember all that you have expected from your cob and don't let that slip – consistency pays! If you always expect your cob to be round and soft then don't let that go now!

Movements based on circles

With the following movements there is more for the rider to do than simply maintain the status quo. Each movement can be described in a series of stages.

10, 12 or 15m half-circles and return to the track
The first part of this movement, the half-circle, is identical to the circle work mentioned above, that is until just before you have reached the halfway mark. In anticipation of that halfway point you need to begin to 'straighten' your cob by asking him to straighten his bend by means of light vibrations with the outside rein against his shoulder. You then

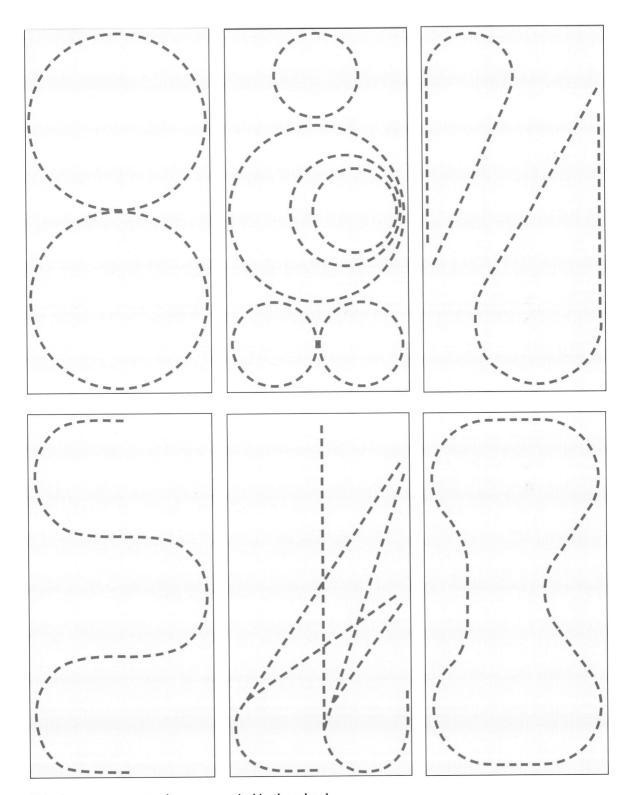

Ride these movements wherever practical in the school.

need to choose a point at which you will return to the track, usually E or B initially, and then later on one of the quarter markers. When on the straight line you will need to keep your cob level in your hands and fairly equal with your legs too. Just before you get to the track you will need to prepare for the new bend. Take things slowly, especially in the changes of bend.

3 and 5m loops in from the track

Remember that change of bend just mentioned? Well, this movement is basically a series of these changes. Start off small, changing from inside bend to outside bend and back again. Then start to bring the loops out a bit bigger. Ask for inside bend coming around the corner. Allow your cob to turn off the track, just 1 or 2m, change the bend slowly to the outside, and turn back to the track and change the bend to the inside again.

I think the key is to remember all of the jobs your hands and legs have to do; it is not just a job for your inside leg, or your inside hand, but a controlled synchronization of actions from your seat, legs and hands that can bring this about. Remember, seat first. This means that, in a change of bend and direction, you will need to change which hip is advancing and which seat bone needs to have more weight (the inside). The inside leg acts forward at the girth to ask for bend from the ribcage while the outside leg stops the cob's hips from pushing out. Of course your reins need to act as mentioned earlier, with the inside slightly raised and flexing to the inside while your outside rein stops the cob's shoulder from pushing out by vibrating against his neck.

Three-loop serpentine

The three-loop serpentine is a progression from the 3 and 5m loops. A three-loop serpentine is a series of three half-circles with two intermediate changes of rein through some straight lines. All that has been mentioned earlier regarding changes of reins should be remembered: particularly remember to bend to the inside through the corner, and continue the bend onto the first half-circle. Straighten your cob for a few strides before changing bend ready for the new half-circle in the other direction. Don't let your cob fall in and remember to ride out to the half-circle before repeating the process to complete the figure.

A little more on bend

I'd like to add a little more about bend here because although a lot of instructors talk about correct bending, very few actually describe it to their pupils in an effective enough way for them to understand fully. Of course your cob needs to look a little to the inside when he is bending in that direction, but this is not the only requirement of correct bend. All this shows is that the cob has flexed his neck. If there is no other bend throughout the body, then it is certain that the cob is only flexing his neck, and as a result he will be falling out through his outside shoulder. As a rider you will feel your cob 'drift out' through his outside shoulder so, despite looking to the inside, he will be moving to the outside.

What I will say is that the bend in your cob needs to appear even throughout his body from poll to tail and if this is the case then, although there will certainly be flexion in your cob's neck, his outside shoulder will not be bulging out. The outside foreleg will not only be swinging forward, but will also stretch more to the inside so that it follows the line of the curve and of the bend.

Another point about correct bend is that this gives both cob and rider the first real feeling of engagement, and the first little glimpses of rudimentary collection, which will not be felt if the bend is not true. I would like you to keep this in mind as the ideal to work towards, but quite often outstanding bend cannot be achieved until the rider has learnt to use the influences of both the shoulder-in and travers to 'wrap the cob' around that inside leg. Early lateral work is discussed in Chapter 6 and this includes a section where I elaborate on the points made here.

Early canter work

Canter in the early stages is best kept outside of the schooling arena or manège. Generally, this canter should be maintained in the forward seat and not on tight turns. However, there comes a point when the canter will need to be worked on in the arena. Nevertheless, I would do no more than make an initial start on this until the point at which the cob is ready to begin some early lateral work because, as mentioned, canter is often the cob's least natural gait (remember most cobs are

A lovely 'airborne' canter with plenty of cadence and suspension.

A view of the canter from the outside of a 20m circle.

bred and built to trot) and he will need the early collection imparted by lateral work to help further in the canter.

When I start initial canter work in the school, I will generally only work on the canter transitions at first, and I will not keep my cobs in canter for any longer than about six or seven strides. This activity is the same as the 'transitions, transitions, transitions concept mentioned earlier. Initially, I will start from trot on a 20m circle but eventually, if

A quality, forward canter during a lap of honour. Great outline is coupled with an 'uphill' way of going and well-engaged hind legs.

not very shortly, I will expect my cob to make some good transitions from walk, as it is these transitions that can really set up the 'uphill', balanced canter which we are looking for.

Let's examine the process in more detail. Starting from a good, well-balanced working trot, ask for a canter transition. Don't let your cob run off in a great big trot but keep the quality while maintaining your canter aids until he pops into canter. If he doesn't and the quality of the trot has been disturbed, return to the walk-trot transitions to re-establish quality and then, the next time you ask for the transition to canter, back up your aid with your schooling whip just behind your inside (dominant) leg and this will usually be enough for the transition to happen. Remember to praise him once the canter has occurred and then make a transition down to trot, re-establish the trot, using some walk transitions if necessary then ask for a canter transition again. Once your cob will 'jump up' into canter when required you can increase the frequency of the canter transitions to six or seven canter strides interspersed by eight to ten strides of trot. Eventually, you can begin to school towards direct transitions from walk to canter. To do this, a similar exercise is required. From walk on a 20m circle, ask for ten strides of trot before asking for canter. Then accept your seven or so canter strides before returning to walk through trot. Repeat this exercise but gradually reduce the number of trot strides between the walk and the canter until eventually you can ask for the canter directly from the walk. I tend to follow this exercise with cobs particularly because of their natural disinclination to canter. This is all I would expect of my cob in canter at this stage, at least until some lateral work is established. Remember to praise all the time your cob is making progress.

For lower-level showing the schooling to this point would be sufficient. But for a higher level, such as county level showing and those who qualify for championships, more refined levels of schooling will be required to enable you to 'have the edge' in the ring.

Long and low stretching work

At regular intervals you will need to allow your cob to stretch his topline forward and down. Never allow him to curl back behind the vertical as this encourages him to hide away from the bit and makes him less likely to seek a contact. At this stage, long and low work can be developed in walk in the rest periods. Ask for the softness in your hands, as explained earlier, then lower you hands on either side of his neck. Once he is soft, allow your hands a little forward with opening

Walk on a loose rein. Allow your cob to stretch forward and down with a slight flexion at the poll.

fingers, then ask again for a little more flexion before allowing with the reins a little more. Each time you do this, feed the reins through your fingers, a little at a time, until your cob's poll is about level with or just below his withers. Your body may incline slightly forward, taking more weight into your thighs and knees, encouraging your cob to lift his back. Your legs keep asking for forward movement alternately with the swing of his belly.

CHAPTER FIVE

An Introduction to Jumping

Cobs are not just underrated in the dressage world! I have found that in many cases their versatility and capabilities in jumping have been ignored – though perhaps to lesser degree than in dressage. You will often see riders competing on their cobs at the lower levels in showjumping, but when it comes the higher levels people are opting for horses with more Thoroughbred blood, such as modern Warmbloods. I remember years ago that in the Junior BSJA shows, most of the top showjumping ponies were small cobs trimmed up. Unfortunately for these little cobs, the fashion for breeding hotter-blooded horses for competition was also followed in the breeding of finer and hotter-blooded ponies.

Also, it's not just at Junior level that 'cobby' types have succeeded. Let's think about Great Britain and Ireland's premier showjumping horses of the 1970s and the 1980s. The Irish Draught is very cobby in type, indeed many of the smaller ones have actually won championships as show cobs, and of course this is a breed that excels in showjumping. Other heavier breeds that have proved their worth in the showjumping arena are the Cleveland Bay and their crosses and Clydesdales and their crosses, and no one can deny the heavy stature of the Clydesdale!

My experience of jumping cobs extends not only to showjumping, but also to cross-country and horse trials and the hunting field. As a child jumping my first pony, a lovely 14.2hh cob mare, I had the advantage of riding a completely unflappable mount, who wasn't at all fazed by bright and spooky fillers. She had the most stylish jump, one that meant she almost never knocked a pole down and, as a result of these two most desirable traits, we were often placed at local shows. Her scope in jumping and her ability to turn quickly meant that as long as we had a double clear we were able to come home with a rosette. In the higher-level classes, her manoeuvrability meant that she was able to cope with the more complex tracks and come home with prizes but, although she could turn quickly her actual speed didn't match her scope for jumping, so although the placings didn't stop, the higher the grade we competed in, the less likely we were to win a class because of the sheer speed necessary to do so. This didn't stop me going though, because it was fun and to achieve any rosette at the higher levels really was something!

As my riding career continued, I came into contact with more and more cobs. A lot of them shared those valuable traits with my first cob Habeabtie. Most of them were unbelievably manoeuvrable, incredibly stylish and very careful. When I was 18, and working with an international event rider, I was asked to ride a lovely bay cob, by the name of Welshman. He had become a little sour in his dressage work and he came to me to start jumping him in a hope that this would broaden his

A lovely cob showing just how talented cobs can be in jumping. Style and scope are great.

horizons and 'put a smile back on his face'. It soon became clear that he loved jumping. Our first outing was a local Riding Club showjumping evening. We were placed in every class we entered! Soon we were con-fident enough to enter a Pre-novice one-day event and came home with a second place! Welshman was a cob who really gave me his heart: we were never unplaced in novice-level hunter trials against horses (jumping up to about 3ft/90cm) and he was even placed in his first open hunter trials, jumping a course of 3ft 6in (106cm).

Ketchup is gymnastically as capable as either Welshman or Hab-eabtie. If anything her technique is better. Her bascule over a fence is excellent and she tends to put a lot of gusto into the lift to her shoulders. She is safe and steady but with plenty of scope. I have jumped her round showjumping tracks of 4ft (120cm) and at that height she is careful, stylish and very consistent.

There is no reason why your cob shouldn't be capable of jumping round courses of decent-sized fences if he has the same capabilities as the cobs just mentioned. I wholeheartedly believe that there should be a greater representation of cobs in all disciplines. Granted, at the higher levels, speed may become an issue, but in the great scheme of things how many horses reach those dizzying heights of advanced/ international level in any particular discipline? So, with that in mind, why don't we see many more cobs competing in the lower levels of BS showjumping, or at Pre-novice and Novice Horse Trials? I really do

Cobs take everything in their stride, even complex combinations into and out of water.

Bold jumping style develops over time using the strategies in this book.

think it is fashion rather than a suitability issue. Many people seem to choose horses with a lot of Thoroughbred blood to compete at these lower levels despite the fact that a good cob would be just as capable at these levels and the rider might well avoid having to cope with a horse of hot temperament! At Riding Club and local level, I have to say you cannot beat the great cob.

I feel that progression in jumping is dependent on basic groundwork. One reason why I have put this chapter in this position is to highlight the fact that basic schooling on the flat, as discussed in the preceding chapters, is an essential prerequisite for successful jumping. I also think, however, that the techniques and exercises discussed in this chapter will complement your dressage schooling in various ways, especially in respect of your cob's canter work. Just as with dressage schooling, jumping has its own prerequisites in terms of rider techniques, so I think that is a good a place as any to start.

Riding and jumping position

There are a number of differences between riding on the flat and over jumps that need to be mentioned. First, we must consider our cob's centre of balance. In dressage riding we have our stirrup leathers rather longer than we would need for jumping because, when working on the flat, our cob's balance is much more stable and so we do not need to adjust our position to the extent that we do during jumping. In order for you to maintain balance with your cob while jumping, I would suggest putting your stirrup leathers up at least three holes. This is especially important if you tend to ride with particularly long leathers when doing dressage. By closing down the angles of your torso to thigh and your thigh to shin, you are ensuring that you are optimally (and most securely) placed to alter your position to suit your cob's balance. Additionally, if you use a dressage saddle for your flatwork, you will probably wish to change to a general-purpose or dedicated jumping saddle for any significant jumping.

So with your stirrup leathers at the shortened length, your 'default' position for jumping will involve you putting more weight into your thighs, through your knees and into your ankles. Have a feeling that your large toes bear more weight than the little toes, thus allowing your knees to come closer into contact with your knee rolls on the saddle. With that weight where it should be, take your shoulders forward and lift your backside out of the saddle – but not too high! Look where you are going and have a feeling that your backside is pointing further back towards the cantle of the saddle. Imagine trying to adopt this position without shortening your leathers! Your thigh to shin angle would be too open for you to adopt a more forward position without 'standing' in your stirrups. When your legs are in such a straight position it is nigh on impossible for you to fold your torso down sufficiently without losing balance. If you jumped in this position you would undoubtedly fall either in front of or back behind the movement, with possibly a later meeting with the ground!

The correct position can be assumed while you walk, trot and canter and I would recommend that you practise this in all gaits with your cob until you can maintain your balance. In trot and in canter you will need to use your ankle, knee and hip joints as your suspension system, absorbing the bounce and rhythm that your cob pushes your way.

When you actually come to do some jumping, you don't need to maintain the jumping position while riding round the arena. It is only necessary for you to maintain a slightly light seat, keeping more weight in your thighs and taking your shoulders ever so slightly more forward. Any of the other advice mentioned in Chapter 2 would apply here. When you ride around a course of jumps in trot, you must guard your 'tick-tock' rhythm, making sure your cob stays energetic and 'in front of your leg'. In canter you need to make sure that he doesn't get so onward that he ends up becoming heavy and on the forehand. Keep the rhythm! As just stated, you only need to adopt the actual jumping position as your cob begins to lift into the jump. You need to feel as though you are 'meeting your cob in the middle'. As he lifts into the jump, you need to take extra weight into your stirrups; as you take your shoulders forward have a feeling that your backside comes up a little out of the saddle and moves back towards the cantle. Think about 'folding down' into your jumping position and following the stretch of your cob's head and neck with your hands rather than jumping forwards yourself.

Early exercises with poles

When you are confident in your balance (control and strength of the position) while riding in the forward jumping seat in all three gaits, you are ready to introduce your cob to some simple pole exercises.

Ground-poles

The first exercise would be simply to have a couple of single poles dotted around your riding area. Start by riding around your arena in the three gaits and, of course, over the poles. Start in walk and, just as you approach each pole, push more weight into your thighs, knees and ankles. Unless your cob is going to jump the pole from walk (or you are unsure of his likely reaction), then this position will be sufficient. If he is likely to jump the pole then adopt a slight jumping position. As he steps (or jumps) the pole, allow your hands forward slightly so he can lower his head sufficiently to look at the pole. Once he is happily walking over the poles in each direction then you should go forward to the trot.

Ride your cob into you forward, regular, working trot rhythm. Keep your rising trot especially soft and allow your hands to maintain a soft, low contact. As you approach the pole take extra care that the rhythm and speed don't alter. If he backs off the pole a little, put your leg on with a little nudge and that should be just enough to encourage him to step over the pole. Again, as he is about to step over the pole, adopt that slightly more forward position and allow your hands a little more forward. If he seems likely to jump the pole, adopt the jumping position just in case. The same goes for the canter. While cantering around the arena, keep the rhythm slow and, if need be, revitalize the gait by making regular transitions through trot and walk. While in canter, maintain the more forward seat. When in that light seat, the jumping position is merely an extension of the existing posture of your body. All you need to do is fold your body down a little lower as his canter stride, or jump, rises up more in front. Remember your shoulders fold down, while your seat lifts up and back.

Once you and your cob are happy with these single poles, you can begin to add sequences of poles. I always begin to add a second pole at a distance of between 8 and 9ft (2.4–2.7m). If your cob's stride is on the short side, start with the lesser distance; if he has a longer stride, try the greater. With poles spaced like this, your cob will make three strides between them in walk, two in trot and he will bounce over each pole if you canter him through. Again, start with walk, and when both of you are happy, proceed to trot. At this point, just be careful that as you approach them he doesn't rush off into canter and bounce over them. Maintain your rhythm, and make sure you allow enough for him to stretch his head and neck forward over the poles – but obviously not

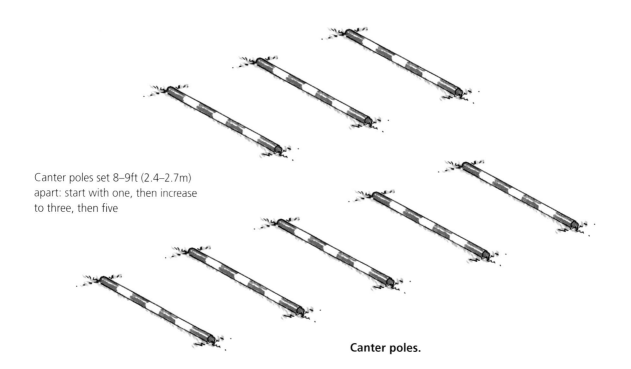

Canter poles set 8–9ft (2.4–2.7m) apart: start with one, then increase to three, then five

Canter poles.

enough to throw all of the energy out of the window. In canter, the balance over your thighs, knees and ankles will become much more important. This allows you to balance over him whatever striding he takes over the poles. At this point, you need to allow him enough room to make his own mistakes. He needs to learn to look after himself and this is where that education starts. So, maintaining the trot initially, as you approach the first pole increase pressure from your legs, and ask him to pop into canter. Let him bounce over the two poles, repeat this a couple of times and then you can have a go at approaching in an established canter. At this point, it is especially important that you maintain a good rhythm. If he runs onto his forehand mistakes will happen more and more.

When you can negotiate these short pole grids happily in walk, trot and canter, you can begin to add more and more poles to the grids at a similar distance to those you have already used.

You can also begin to develop 'trotting poles' by starting off with your two poles set at the 8–9ft (2.4–2.7m) distance. When you are confident that you can trot through these poles quietly and your cob is

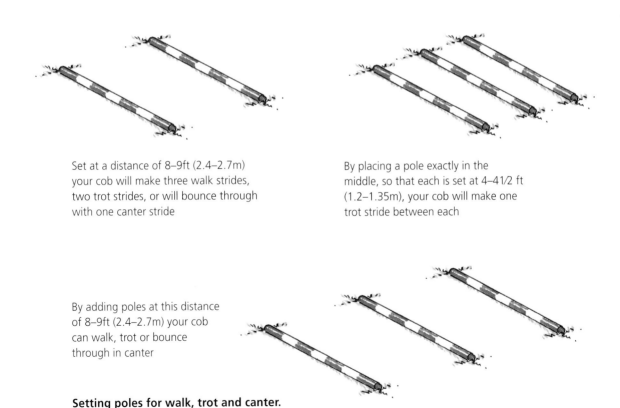

Set at a distance of 8–9ft (2.4–2.7m) your cob will make three walk strides, two trot strides, or will bounce through with one canter stride

By placing a pole exactly in the middle, so that each is set at 4–4½ ft (1.2–1.35m), your cob will make one trot stride between each

By adding poles at this distance of 8–9ft (2.4–2.7m) your cob can walk, trot or bounce through in canter

Setting poles for walk, trot and canter.

maintaining his rhythm well (and doesn't canter off unless asked), you can add a third pole exactly in the middle. When the poles are thus set about 4–4½ft (1.2–1.35m) apart, you will feel an increased cadence in your cob's stride, with greater definition to his hoofbeats as he articulates all of his joints to step over each pole in sequence. You will feel that you will need to rise slightly higher and longer as he steps over the poles and it is most important here that you maintain your lower hand position through the poles so he can maintain the stretch in his head and neck.

The first cross-pole

Once the preliminary pole exercises are well established, and you have confidence in your balance in the forward seat, you can confidently tackle the following exercise. Start off with two poles at your cob's preferred distance between 8 and 9ft (2.4–2.7m). Start by trotting through the poles in both directions. When you are both happy you can choose your preferred direction (although you will do this exercise on both reins in due course) and add a pair of wings and another pole to the second pole in the sequence, so that you convert the second pole to a small cross-pole. Approach this simple grid in an active and rhythmical trot. As you approach the first pole (that on the ground), keep your leg nudging your cob forward. Try to give him enough leg just before the first pole so that he bounces over this and jumps cleanly over the cross-pole. The first pole is called a placing pole and it does exactly that; it positions your cob in the correct place for take-off over the second. As well as making it easier for him, it lets you know when to adopt your jumping position, so just after the bounce over the placing pole, as he lifts into his jump, adopt the jumping position. Try to return to the light seat as soon as you land, without being too abrupt, but also without letting yourself peck forward onto your cob's shoulders. Once you are happy with your initial jumps, try putting your little grid in different places in the arena, and make sure you do it on both reins. You can increase the height of your cross-poles, but I would recommend that, initially, you stick to cross-poles as these will guide your cob to the middle of all of the jumps.

Starting doubles with poles.

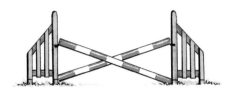

Start by trotting through two poles set at 8–9ft (2.4–2.7m) apart

When comfortable, replace the second pole with a small cross-pole at 8–9ft (2.4–2.7m)

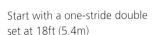

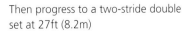

Start with a one-stride double set at 18ft (5.4m)

Then progress to a two-stride double set at 27ft (8.2m)

Early gridwork

I always recommend that, at this stage, a rider concentrates much more on gridwork than on working towards jumping a course of showjumps. That is purely because gridwork really prepares you and your cob for the technicalities of jumping more complex courses. It develops your cob's balance and really gets him to think a little more for himself and to work out where his limbs are at any one time. These are prerequisites for your cob getting himself out of sticky situations while negotiating complex courses, whether showjumping or cross-country.

So, once you and your cob are both happy with these single jump grids you can begin to increase the number of jumps that you tackle in longer and longer sequences. I generally start with a simple one-stride double. Starting on your preferred rein, begin with the simple placing pole to a cross-pole. Once you have been over this a couple of times, introduce a single pole on the ground about 18ft (5.4m) after the cross-pole. Go through your grid again. After your first jump, sit up slightly using your upper body to balance yourself before allowing with your hands over the new pole and, if necessary, be prepared to adopt a more forward jumping position. You may need to adjust the distance between the cross-pole and the second pole depending on your cob's stride. When you are happy you can add another pole and convert that ground-pole to a second cross-pole. Now, you will need to adapt your position quickly and at the right moment. Remember, though, in the middle (non-jumping) stride to sit up a little and nudge a little with your legs to maintain impulsion.

Once successful, another one-stride element can be added onto this simple grid in exactly the same way. Be sure, however, that both of you are comfortable with what you have been doing, and that you are able to maintain your balance absolutely without faltering. Since your cob may gain momentum and stride length throughout the grid, you may need to extend the distance of the second element a little, but make sure you don't extend it too much as this will result in him flattening. However, if you have followed the procedure outlined, you will hopefully have found out what distance suits your cob best anyway.

Of course, you don't need to limit yourself to one-stride grids. Two strides are just as feasible in between two jumps. Making sure that you only approach the grid in trot, the distance for two strides would be about 27ft (8.2m). You can extend the sequence from two jumps set at two strides apart, to three jumps two strides apart. Again, at this early stage, you should just stick to simple cross-poles as guides for your cob to travel through the middle of the jumps. However, you can also mix and match the distances. For example, start with a single-stride distance and follow this with a two-stride gap, perhaps reversing this at a later stage. See the diagrams in this chapter for more gridwork ideas.

Once you and you cob are confident with the cross-pole grids, you can begin to change the style of the jumps. You can introduce some upright jumps, so long as they have a drop pole underneath and a ground-pole ever so slightly in front of the drop pole. Later on, as we shall see, you can also incorporate some simple spread fences into your grids, adjusting the distances as necessary; initially the front part could simply be a cross-pole while you could put a simple straight bar behind it set at about a distance of 2ft (60cm) away from the cross, making sure the back pole is a somewhat higher than the cross. (Or you could use a front upright with a slightly higher back pole.)

The important thing when designing your grids is to make sure that the first fence is the smallest, the last is the highest and each fence in between is set at, at least, the same height as the preceding one. At no time should the following fence be smaller. When approaching the grid it is important to maintain the rhythm of the trot before the placing pole. The trot needs to be active and forward but certainly not rushing. The key, once you reach the placing pole, is to push your cob forward suitably, sitting up well in between the jumps and allowing your cob plenty of room to stretch over them by making sure your hands follow the forward movement of his head and neck.

The first showjumping course

The gridwork completed to date has laid the foundations for you and your cob to start jumping short courses of single jumps. It has shown your cob where his legs are, has taught him how long his strides are and has also taught him to see his own strides.

You can approach the beginning of course-jumping in one of two ways. The first is by dotting single cross-poles around the school, each with its own placing pole, and riding each one at trot. Or you can ride through a simple grid a couple of time to set your cob up then,

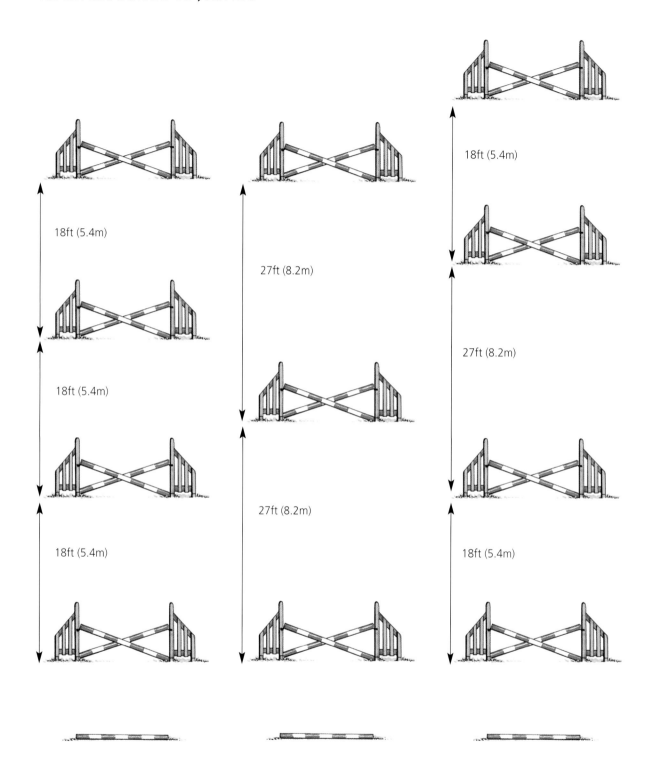

Constructing early grids.

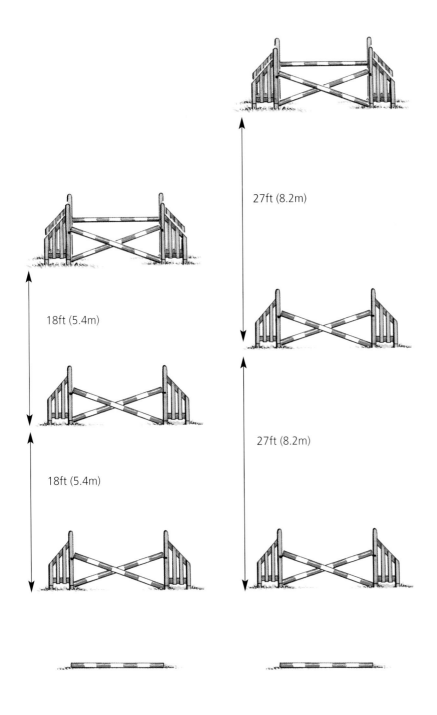

27ft (8.2m)

18ft (5.4m)

18ft (5.4m)

27ft (8.2m)

maintaining a rhythmical forward canter in a slightly forward seat, you can proceed around the school to a simple cross-pole or upright fence with a ground-pole (but not a placing pole). In the latter case, maintain your light seat with pulsing legs, aim for the middle of the single fence and, when your cob makes his jump, remember to fold and 'meet him in the middle' with your jumping position. On landing remember to sit up, accept a few strides of canter then ride forwards to walk and reward. If your cob backs off the fence and refuses to go forward, increase your leg aids and, if need be, give him a tap with the whip, but if your preparation so far has been thorough this should not happen.

Base all your early work on the simple grid, and then build up to short, simple courses incorporating turns and changes of rein, always maintaining rhythm, forwardness, and a light seat, being ready to fold and meet your cob in a jumping position over the fence. Be positive with your riding and ride to the middle of all of your fences. If your cob gets too heavy, too onward or unruly, make a transition to trot or walk and start again. Don't make your courses too complex and, most of all, reward all of your cob's efforts. Make sure both of you have fun.

More advanced jumping

Advancement in jumping is as progressive as the training in dressage, so although a lot of what follows is dependent on your cob having worked through many of the flatwork exercises described in the next two chapters, you may start some of these exercises earlier than others depending on your achievements at home. Obviously, discretion is necessary here because, although correct jumping can complement flatwork, no horse's flatwork will improve suddenly just because he is confronted by some fences. For example, for some of these exercises, early collection is necessary so that your cob has sufficient suppleness, manoeuvrability, and power to cope with the more complex techniques. Therefore, always be mindful of your cob's level of training on the flat when undertaking jumping exercises.

These techniques discussed here are those that I have used extensively with all types of horses, but they work extremely well with horses of heavier build. I believe they are perfect for cobs because, although they are forward-going rides when allowed to be so, they very rarely become the sharp, excitable mounts that horses with a lot of Thoroughbred blood can so easily become. These techniques serve to sharpen up your cob's jumping technique, without making riding him difficult or unmanageable. (With 'sharper' horses you tend to have the difficulty of riding round a course trying to maintain control and rhythm and then, when you get to the jump, you then have to find ways to control the exuberance and size of the effort, never mind the developing technique.)

Advancing with gridwork

More advanced gridwork involves slightly shortening or lengthening distances between the fences. It also involves incorporating slightly bigger fences and those with a slightly more complicated structure, designed to develop your cob's bascule. Some of these more advanced techniques also help to develop cadence, height and roundness of the canter stride.

Grids with ground 'stride' poles

The first step in progressing towards more advanced gridwork is to start with a simple one-stride double and put a ground-pole equal distance between the two fences. These ground-poles serve to round up your cob's back, lower his neck and engage his hind legs further under his body in order to put more style and technique into the following jump. When your cob has a rounded back and a slightly lower neck just before the jump, then as long as you ask for enough energy with your legs, he should spring up with his shoulders, round his frame over the fence and jump with a technique that is more 'economical' on the body; a more biomechanically safe way that will look after his musculature and joint system.

Start with your placing pole on the floor, a small cross-pole between 8 and 9ft (2.4–2.7m) after it, then place another pole on the floor following the fence set at the same distance as your placing pole. This simple start helps to lower your cob's head so that he rounds his back over the fence. Once you have jumped through this mini grid from a forward, rhythmical trot in both directions you can begin to add more fences. Begin by adding another simple cross-pole set again at the same distance as before (the same height too). If you place a pole on the ground following this second fence at the same distance, then you

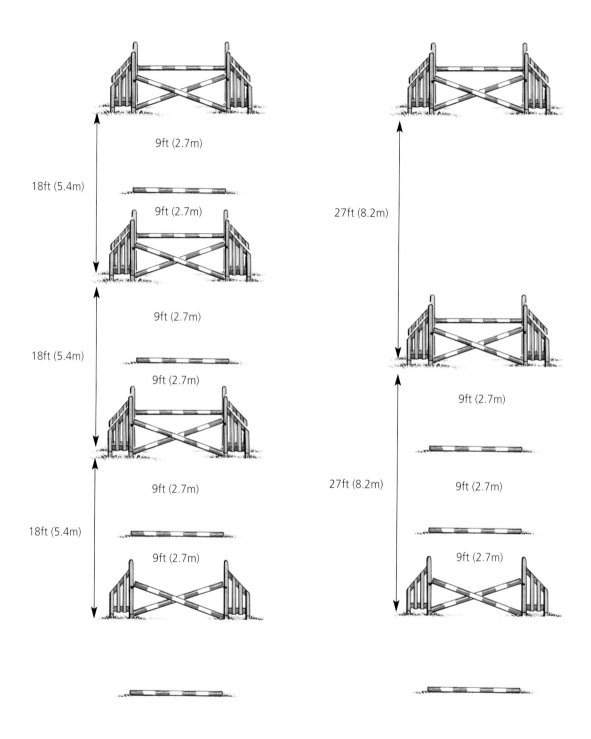

9ft (2.7m)

18ft (5.4m)

9ft (2.7m)

27ft (8.2m)

9ft (2.7m)

18ft (5.4m)

9ft (2.7m)

9ft (2.7m)

18ft (5.4m)

9ft (2.7m)

27ft (8.2m)

9ft (2.7m)

9ft (2.7m)

**More advanced gridwork, incorporating ground-poles
and spread fences to make your grids more complex.**

will be able to jump through this grid on both reins. You can add more and more fences in this way – though don't overface your cob!

The same process can be used for grids with two strides between the fences. Each stride, however, needs its own pole on the ground, so for two fences set in a distance of 27ft (8.2m), you would set two poles into that distance at 9ft (2.7m) and then again at 18ft (5.4m). Of course, if your cob needs a shorter or longer distance then the poles need to be set at regular distances within it. Once you are happy with both the one-stride and two-stride grids, you can further develop sharpness in your cob's technique by mixing and matching the two. For example, start with a placing pole, 9ft (2.7m) to a cross pole, the same distance to a ground pole, then to a second cross-pole, followed by a two-stride gap with poles after 9ft (2.7m) and 18ft (5.4m), followed by a third fence after 27ft (8.2m). You can then add another pole at 9ft (2.7m) from that fence and a final one after another 9ft (2.7m). Other ideas for these grids can be seen in the illustrations.

Shortening and lengthening the stride in gridwork

To start working towards a shorter stride, I always recommend that you start with a simple grid with two fences set at one stride apart. A placing pole starts the grid, and a ground-pole needs to be placed between the two fences as described earlier. When shortening the stride between fences you should never shorten the whole thing by more than a few inches at a time. Pull the ground-pole back by about 3in (7–8cm), and then the second fence can be pulled back by about 6in (15cm). See how your cob copes with this and then you can adjust further grids in a similar process.

Shortening the stride puts a bit more spring into it; your cob's back rounds up further as his hind legs engage a little more under his body. His neck, kept free, is used to allow him to counterbalance by stretching forward and down. By shortening the stride slightly you are basically giving him less room, making him snap his legs up that bit quicker and raise his shoulders higher in a more of a bascule.

I would always recommend that you teach your cob to shorten his stride in gridwork before you move on to lengthening the stride because, by shortening the stride, you are giving him more 'impulsion' in his joints. I think of it as akin to teaching collection in dressage before you teach the extensions. Indeed, the collection is a prerequisite of extension. Those engaged and flexed hind legs that epitomise collection are so necessary in producing extensions, and this is mirrored in jumping. Once his hind legs are engaging more for jumping, he will be able to use this quality to take the stride forward in balance, without pushing onto the forehand.

To start working towards a longer stride, as with shortening, I recommend that you start with a simple grid with two fences set one stride apart. When lengthening the stride between two fences you should only do so about the same amount that you would shorten it, that is, no more than a few inches at a time. Pull the ground-pole forward by about 3in (7–8cm) and then the second fence can be pulled forward by about 6in (15cm). Remember that your cob needs to cover more ground per stride so 'allow' a little more through your body, through your rising in the trot and through the contact to the bit. As you ride through the grid, apply a little more leg; see how he responds and how he copes with this longer stride. By expecting him to lengthen the stride slightly you are basically testing his manoeuvrability and response to your aids, making him stretch a little more forward through his shoulders, neck and back. As with the shortening, once you are happy with the simple grid, the principle can be extended to more complex constructions.

Grids with bigger fences and more complex build pattern

These are introduced to further develop the cob's bascule. I generally use these fences in grids with a normal striding, though at times I would consider putting some into the grids with a slightly shorter stride distance if I feel that my cob needs more challenge to develop a better style. Generally speaking, I don't put anything other than simple crosses and basic spread fences into the grids with a slightly lengthened stride distance.

Once I have introduced ground-poles between jumps within a grid, I rarely go without them. I start off with a simple grid of three cross-poles set one stride apart, introduced by a placing pole and with ground-poles in between. I then increase the height of the second and third fences. Generally speaking, high cross-poles improve technique by giving your cob a narrower channel to jump through, with little room for dangling legs. This encourages him to snap up his legs and shoulders while lowering his neck and rounding his back more. (As the height of cross-poles increases up the jump wings, you will notice that the middle part of the cross doesn't get too high, but the sloping poles either side get quite high quite quickly – this is the tunnel I'm referring to.)

Once you and your cob are both used to these high-sided cross-poles in your grids you can further develop this by adding a back pole about 2ft (60cm) from the cross (remember that, when adding a back pole, the distances in the grids need to be altered to accommodate the added spread). Eventually you can begin to heighten the back pole, at the same time as pulling out the spread of the jump. Later on in your training you can replace the back pole with another cross-pole of identical size and proportions to the front one. Again, these can be pulled out to increase the spread, remembering to alter your distances in the grids according to the spreads of the fences you use. Upright parallel fences with a back pole (the same height as the front one) that is pulled out to an increased distance can have a similar effect. Stretching out the spread in these fences really encourages various qualities in your cob's jump. While stretching his back and further lowering his neck, it makes him much sharper with his technique, making him look at his fence, work out what to do with his limbs and learn to extend his jump from a shorter stride base.

Using ground-poles to improve the canter

Once the cob has reached this stage in his education, to develop the canter for gridwork (see below) and other purposes I begin to use poles on the ground one canter stride apart. I start off establishing the canter on the circle, then I take the cob large around the arena where I have some poles laid out at a distance of 2.4–2.7m (8–9ft) apart. Initially of course I start with one pole, then I will increase this to three then five poles. When I go over the poles I adopt a forward seat, taking more weight in my knees and into my stirrups as this will give the cob much more freedom. Once arriving at the far end of the arena I make a transition to trot, and then start the exercise again. This exercise can be extended by raising the poles off the ground and can even be extended into 'bounce' jumps. This really gives bascule to the whole canter stride. It raises the cob's back and really gives 'jump' to the canter stride, a truly wonderful feeling. I still use this exercise to freshen up Ketchup's canter to good effect; it's a great way to get an 'uphill' canter without feeling as though you have to resort to stronger aiding!

Gridwork from canter

All of the gridwork mentioned earlier can be ridden from an approach in canter as well as trot. The differences are in the absence of a placing pole (this being replaced by a ground-pole at the base of the first fence), and by lengthening the distance between the fences. As your approach will now be in a more onward-bound stride, the stride length at the start of the grid will be much longer, so it is inevitable that the stride length between the fences will also be longer (add about 30cm/2ft per stride within the grid – but check how this rides for your cob, and adjust if necessary).

The key to cantering through a grid is to establish the canter well before you approach the grid. It can be useful to practise this at first to a single jump. Maintaining a rhythmical, forward canter in a slightly forward seat, you could ride around the school to a simple cross-pole or an upright fence with a ground-pole (but not a placing pole). Maintain your light seat with pulsing legs, aim for the middle of this first fence and when your cob makes his jump remember to fold and 'meet him in the middle' with your jumping position. On landing remember to sit up for a few strides of canter; keep your leg on and when riding to the next element and, if he backs off, you may need to give him a tap with the whip. Once this practice is successful, base your early canter gridwork on riding in the same style. Be positive with your riding and ride to the middle of all of your grids.

Improving the canter for jumping

There will come a time when simply setting off into a canter rhythm, maintaining a light seat will not be enough to improve your cob's jumping technique to the desired standard. The canter used for jumping increasingly complex tracks with larger fences needs to be somewhat different from that ridden in your flatwork – or at least a development from it. That said, the work in canter in your dressage schooling will have suppled and gymnasticized your cob, preparing him for this work. Without that as your foundation the following strategies will be impossible.

I remember getting quite hung up about being able to see a stride. In my attempts to see the strides to the fences, I started holding Ketchup back rather than riding her forward. Despite the fact that many instructors, riding manuals and instructional videos had told me to ride a rhythmical canter, I couldn't get over my hang-up. It wasn't until a friend of mine, an Advanced event rider, had watched me ride Ketchup, seen my problems, and told me to think about getting Ketchup 'rearing up at me in canter' that things really came together. What she was basically saying was that, really, rhythm isn't quite enough. You need a strong rhythm that is being actively contained so as to produce a ground-eating stride that can be shortened or lengthened at will. By having that ground-eating, 'uphill' stride your cob always has the power to jump, whether he arrives at the fence close, or further away. When Sandra told me to get Ketchup 'rearing up at me in canter' she didn't mean to have her hollow, but to have the canter stride 'jumping up in front', with more expression. I now ride with this in my mind on all horses, and I have to say it works beautifully with the cobs.

To achieve this feeling, first strike-off into the canter, but rather than going into the light seat that we have been using to date, stay in the full seat. Your legs need to become much more 'demanding' rather than 'asking'. Put your leg on and expect a reaction from your cob; he should feel that he wants to go more forward. This forward impulse is contained by the 'holding' aid, of your seat, back and your abdominal muscles. Your will need to back this up with a feel and vibration on the outside rein. As described in the later chapters dealing with piaffe and advanced canter exercises, it becomes important that your cob maintains a higher centre of balance when preparing his canter for more advanced jumping. This is achieved simply by raising your hand gently and with caution for a few moments while asking your cob to 'step' a little with your legs (try not to change the balance by using the hands harshly or on their own); guard against him speeding up by adding extra tone in your body and vibrating more on the outside rein. Wait until he has stepped a little more forward with his hind legs in a more active canter and is stepping a bit higher with his forehand. When this happens, stop and praise him before repeating the exercise. Just as in the piaffe, by maintaining this raised carriage you are guarding against him falling onto his forehand, which could be so easy in this more forward, ground-eating canter; it guards against him from falling onto your hands, and also from dropping the impulsion already built into the canter.

Once you have attained this 'ground-eating' canter, there are several exercises you can do with it, to prepare yourself and your cob for tackling bigger courses.

Improving style and bascule

High cross-poles

We start with high cross-poles. Having set up the canter as described above, choose a line which will take you straight over the centre of the fence. Make sure there is enough room to take four or five straight canter strides either side of it. Once your canter is set up, sit in your full seat and canter straight to the fence. In the last few strides your hands will need to soften a little to allow your cob to lower his head. This sets him up for a well-basculed jump by putting him in the best position to snap his legs up, push his shoulders up, round his back and stretch out over the fence. The very last stride before take-off is a

A young cob showing just how hard he is trying for his rider.
Good bascule shown here.

crucial moment in this process; this is when you need to give him even more room with your hands. By giving him room, I do not mean that you should 'drop him' (lose the contact), I mean give him room to stretch forward. At the same moment you will need to nudge him with more leg and it is this combined push forwards with the room to stretch in his neck that allows him to develop bascule. As mentioned earlier, these high cross-poles create that image of a tunnel for your cob to travel through and thus encourage him to snap up his forelegs just a little bit quicker.

High cross/spread fences

The cross-poles used above can be further developed in a similar way to the progression in gridwork. A second set of poles can be duplicated about 2ft (60cm) behind the original fence. Gradually, you can pull out these cross-poles further apart, making the spread wider and wider. The widening spread encourages a much rounder back as well as an increased lowering of the neck over the fence. This exercise thus encourages cobs who don't naturally have a bascule in their jump to develop a more stylish technique. For others, it creates a more pronounced bascule which will allow cobs of even average ability to achieve excellent jumping results. Your cob may be reluctant on the approach to this type of fence initially and, if this is the case, stay positive with your legs,

A cob showing good scope over a triple bar.

and back them up with your whip if necessary. However, if the training so far has been progressive, building confidence and technique and not overfacing the cob, this should not happen.

Wide parallels

Similarly to the high and wide cross-poles mentioned above, these spread fences need to be approached in the strong, ground-eating canter, and in the approach you will need to allow you cob 'breathing space'. That is, don't overload your aiding. Then, in the last couple of strides, ease your contact a little thus allowing that stretch in the neck. In the last stride, allow a little more with the hands while, at the same time, pulsing with your leg for an extra bit of lift. These wider parallel fences encourage a much rounder back when met correctly, as well as more stretching forward and lowering of the neck through the jump. This creates more a refinement of the bascule, giving more scope to your cob's jumping.

Fences with tramlines

These are basically simple upright fences with drop poles and a ground line. A pole is positioned on the top pole at an angle to the ground either side of centre. These fences are another way of creating the image of jumping through a tunnel and thus encourage straight jumping. The tramline poles encourage your cob to be very careful with his forelegs and to push up through the shoulders. Gradually, you can make the angle of the poles on the top pole narrower so that they almost meet in a point. Later on, as you and your cob become more accustomed to this style of jump, you can combine these tramlines with the wide parallel fences mentioned above. As with the high cross/ spread fences your cob may back off on the approach to this type of fence initially and if this is the case stay positive with your legs, and back them up with your whip if necessary. However, this problem is less likely to occur if the tramlines are placed pretty wide initially, and the angle only reduced gradually, once the cob is confident.

The work on jumping so far would be the kind of work that would help develop a show jumping cob as well as those who participate in working cob classes which include jumping (rather like working hunters but for cobs). They also proved the basis for cross-country riding. They develop flexibility, quickness of thinking, and most of all, rhythm. For your early cross-country efforts sit forward in your light/jumping seat and develop the rhythm that your cob sets. When settled, head for your first couple of fences. Look forward past the fences and keep the rhythm. I think you'll be amazed by how much easier cross-country riding and jumping actually is!

....

CHAPTER SIX

Early Lateral Work and Its Benefits

In-hand beginnings

The first step in teaching your cob some of the early lateral movements is in-hand work. In Chapter 4 we discussed the position you should be in when you are working your cob in-hand and that position should be maintained throughout your in-hand work, except for some slight variations discussed within this current chapter. I should say that I would use these methods with all horses and ponies because if you first introduce your mount to the lateral movements (especially the more complex ones) in-hand, he will usually understand far sooner when the exercise is introduced in his ridden repertoire. This method also allows the intelligent rider/trainer to bypass some of the more common confusions and frustrations that are often associated with the teaching of lateral work.

Respect for the basic aids

The very first step is to teach your cob not to invade your space and to respect your body language by teaching him to stop and go from the slightest of aids and later on to establish the rein-back in his in-hand work. So, to reiterate your in-hand position, standing on the left, your left hand is on the left rein very close to the bit ring and your right hand is holding the schooling whip and the right rein, which has been brought over your cob's neck and withers and is positioned level to where the girth would be if your cob were saddled up. (Of course these exercises must be done from both sides of your cob; the above position is for the trainer standing on the nearside, (left) of the horse.)

The aid for your cob to move forwards is to raise the schooling whip in your left hand from low down to the level of his quarters while saying 'walk on'. Make sure your rein contact is kept soft because, if you are heavy on the reins, or you allow your cob to push on the reins, he is likely to continue pushing through your hands when you are asking for a transition to halt. So, to ask for a halt transition I tend to make sure that the reins stay soft, I'll then give a few extra vibrations on the rein and, rather than directing my body forwards, I'll turn to face more to the rear of the cob, and I'll slow my walk right down until the cob is standing in a halt. Of course, praise must follow a correct response so that your cob knows he has done what was expected of him, and the more you do this exercise the more responsive he will become to these aids.

It really didn't take Ketchup long to read my body language. Soon, I would only need to think 'halt' and Ketchup would be halted, looking very proud of herself. However, some cobs – those who haven't necessarily been taught appropriate boundaries – may try to barge and run onto their trainer's hand. I will always remember a lovely big black cob called Paddy. He loved people but was unfortunate that all his owners lacked confidence and so he took charge of most situations, not out of desire but out of necessity. He came to my yard and tried to walk over everyone. Within half an hour of his first in-hand schooling session, Paddy had stopped running onto my hand and had stopped trying to barge over the top of me. I followed the same procedure as above but as soon as he tried to barge I would push onto the noseband of the cavesson he was wearing to stop him and make him step back. It worked a treat and with this renewed respect, schooling proper could begin.

This type of rein-back activity will, in fact, benefit any cob as it will help to flex the joint systems in his hind legs and lighten his forehand. So, once the cob is halted, I point towards his shoulder with the word 'back' and, if need be, put my hand on his shoulder and apply light pulsing pressure until he steps back with one foot, remembering to praise him and repeat, always lightening the aids the more I do it, so that eventually he will step back from a mere point of the finger or from a simple voice aid 'back'. Along with the lateral movements the rein-back is the key to collection and is an essential ingredient in teaching much more advanced movements, such as piaffe.

First lateral steps in-hand

Using what we have taught our cob so far, the next step is to take the bend developed initially in-hand (see Chapter 4) onto a circle and to send it a little bit sideways. So, start in the 'default' in-hand position as described earlier. From the bending exercise on the circle, where you were flexing your cob a little to the inside making sure he didn't push onto his inside shoulder, put your right hand a little way behind the girth. Continue on the line you were following and, with your right hand behind the girth, push a little more with the swing of the belly. This is usually enough to send your cob a little bit sideways with his hindquarters. You will need to make sure that he still bends well to the inside, that he doesn't push too much weight onto his outside shoulder, nor does he fall in and spin his quarters out. If he does any of these things, slow down, as they usually happen when too much emphasis is put on the sideways movement alone.

If your cob doesn't move his hindquarters sideways from the pulsing pressure of your inside hand behind the girth, you can synchronize your whip aid on his thigh with the hand aid on his side. (This happens when his hind leg is off the ground and is swinging forward.) The moment your cob responds by stepping away from the pressure of your hand or the combined aids of hand and whip, praise him immediately. At this stage it is more than sufficient for your cob to step out with his hind legs to the point where his inside hind leg steps on the same track of the circle as his outside foreleg. With time, your cob will supple up to the stage where he will be able to describe a 4 or 5m circle while crossing both his fore and hind legs. This movement, which is called the giravolta, should of course be practised equally on both reins, and is the ultimate in suppling up any horse. Of course, the more you practise these movements the lighter your aids should become and eventually they will become invisible to the onlooker and you will appear to read the mind of your cob as he reads yours.

Leg-yielding in-hand

From the giravolta pretty much on the spot, with you moving your cob over and around a very small circle, you can then 'take a walk' with your cob moving sideways. For example, if you have been doing the giravolta you can then choose to move your cob forwards and sideways on an oblique line where both the forelegs and the hind legs have to cross just as much as each other. (Up until now, with the giravolta, the hind legs have been doing most of the crossing.) This progression is really very simple to do. From the giravolta you need to pick a point on the outside track of the school at which to direct your body language. Move towards it with forward and sideways steps yourself. Make sure you maintain the aids with your hand on your cob's side with the swing of his belly and, if need be, back them up with the tickle from your whip on his thigh when that hind leg is swinging forwards. If he forgets to take his forehand over it is often because your body language isn't 'assertive' enough in moving his shoulders over. You may need to move your pulsing hand onto the shoulders to help move them over while using the end of the whip on his barrel to move his body over with his shoulders. Try to make sure he doesn't rush over to the side too much. It is much better for him to move in a slower walk, which will help to strengthen and supple his muscles, than to move at speed, where he will use the momentum to 'fall' sideways without control.

Shoulder-in in-hand

From the giravolta and the leg-yielding in-hand you can develop the shoulder-in in-hand. This is the first movement that will really introduce true collection. Shoulder-in demands much more true bend than the leg-yield. In the leg-yield you just need your cob to have light flexion in the poll, while the shoulder-in requires bend all through his body.

So, once your cob is capable of the giravolta and the leg-yielding in-hand and on both reins from increasingly light aids, then it is safe to say he is ready for shoulder-in exercises in-hand. Once you have practised a couple of leg-yields in each direction, you can then position your cob on one of the long sides of the school. Stay in halt for a moment and ask for some flexion to the inside. Assuming that you are

Here, I'm showing horse and rider what shoulder-in really is. It is often easier for a rider to feel shoulder-in in this way before being asked to ride it alone. Horses often understand the lateral movements better if they are prepared in-hand first.

on the left rein, position your right hand on the girth (not behind it as in the leg-yield, since we are now asking for bend) and once you have asked for walk you will need to pulse your hand a little with each swing of the belly, as the hind leg on the left side swings forward. Keep the speed fairly slow, keep the flexion to the inside and keep the rein in the right hand vibrating across his neck and shoulder from his offside. Make sure your body allows your cob enough room for his shoulders to move off the track, so consciously remain stepping onto the inner track as you don't want his shoulders to be pushed onto the outer track – in fact you want them to step in a little. Uniform bend is needed through-out his body so make sure your cob keeps looking a little to the inside and, above all, make sure he stays soft and light. Every now and then you can glance back at the tracking your cob is making with his hind legs and hopefully you will find that his inside hind hoof is on the same track as his outside fore hoof – but don't get too obsessed with this as it can often make the trainer lose focus and then the cob is often put under more pressure than necessary. What is more important is the bend through his body.

A note from experience

Ketchup thoroughly enjoys lateral work both in-hand and ridden. From a trainer's point of view, in-hand work really allows you to 'see' what you are doing and you are close enough to influence your cob instantly if things go wrong. At first, Ketchup often didn't have enough true bend in her shoulder-in and it wasn't until we started doing a lot of practice in-hand that we could really influence what her body was doing. She used to step out with her hind legs rather then bend through her body and bring her forehand in. In the in-hand work the focus with Ketchup was less on the sideways-driving effect of the pulsing hand (or the inside leg if ridden) but much more on its bending influence and the lightness of the shoulders. In-hand giravolta and then leg-yield and shoulder-in really transformed Ketchup into a light, responsive athlete. Ketchup's forte now is her lateral work and it really is amazing how these movements have improved her suppleness and gaits no end.

Ridden lateral work

Leg-yielding in walk

Once your cob has mastered leg-yielding in-hand you can attempt the exercise under saddle. I always start in walk and I always take it slowly! I generally start on the rein that the cob finds easier in-hand, and will usually turn down the three-quarter line and leg-yield out towards the track. My aids for the leg-yield ridden are very similar to the in-hand aids except, of course, that the driving aid of the hand is replaced by the inside leg.

First of all make sure you start off are sitting squarely, with even weight between your two seat bones. Make sure your body is guarding against your cob barging forwards too much. Your outside rein needs to stay fairly low against the withers and is used in a vibration. The inside rein is carried slightly higher and, with a vibration, keeps the cob flexed a little to the inside. The inside leg is positioned a little behind the girth and, as always, is used with the swing of the belly, that is when the hind leg is swinging forwards. By thinking about the position of your inside leg, you actually bring the inside hip and seat bone a little further back and, as a result, you advance the outside seat bone and therefore you are well placed in the saddle to move your cob out away from your inside leg. By advancing the outside seat bone you are using an effective weight aid which encourages your cob to move out and under that weight. This, coupled with the driving inside leg, makes it clear which direction your cob should yield to. This alignment is enhanced if you use the leg in time with the swing of the belly as this will advance your outside hip at exactly the right time. The outside leg helps with general activity and can 'catch' the quarters if they get pushed over too far.

Initially, one or two steps will suffice and of course with praise, your cob will soon fully understand what is required of him. Gradually you can expect your cob to maintain these lateral steps for longer and further, from the centre line to the track and even from quarter marker to quarter marker across the diagonal of the school.

One thing that I will emphasize is the need keep things slow. With Ketchup I often felt that I was making halt transitions in between each individual step; this gave me time to co-ordinate the aids and gave Ketchup time to think about what was being asked of her.

One major fault that riders often seem unaware of when riding the leg-yield is that their mounts tend to give far too much bend; they are then well placed to 'escape' through the outside shoulder and trail with their quarters. To correct this I vibrate the fingers on my outside rein, and I use it a little more against the withers; this helps to straighten the neck. Also, I will often use my whip on the quarters at the same time as I use my leg with the swing of the belly. The whip serves to bring the hindquarters in line with the rest of the body. The use of the whip should in no way be aggressive; it should be used in the same way as described in the in-hand work. This is often a great tool for those cobs who have learned this exercise in-hand as they fully understand what the whip aids are requesting.

Lovely crossing from Smokey. Look at his crossing hind leg and his foreleg that is just about to lift. However, Sarah has opened her outside rein far too much. This puts Smokey at risk of falling through his left shoulder. It hasn't happened yet, but it could.

Leg-yielding in trot

Ridden leg-yield in trot can proceed once leg-yielding in walk is fully established. I usually ride leg-yield in rising trot in the very early stages as this generally keeps the cob's back nice and loose. Normally, in the early stages, I will start with the same exercise as described in walk: I will turn my cob down the three-quarter line and leg-yield out to the track for two or three steps. In rising trot I apply my inside leg during the sitting phase of each stride. My hands work in the same way as described for walk. My hips remain central during the sitting phase, but my outside hip points more forward during the rising phase in order to take my weight in the direction that I want to go.

As with walk, keep the trot slow. Remember that too much speed will mean that your cob will merely 'fall' sideways and therefore the gymnastic quality of the leg-yielding will be negated. I will often ride a circle just before starting the leg-yield, and I will work on slowing the trot even more. Then, at each stride after the turn onto the three-quarter or centre line, I work my seat and tone my abdominal muscles in order to slow the stride whilst asking for the sideways movement from my leg. Remember, it is not the hand that slows the trot; this will just make your cob hollow, hide away behind the bit or eventually push hard onto your hand and therefore fall onto the forehand.

Once your cob fully accepts your weight in sitting trot, and you have perfected your sitting trot technique, you can begin to develop leg-yielding in sitting trot. The aids are exactly the same as in walk. Your seat acts in exactly the same way; inside leg applied with the swing of the belly, which will advance your outside hip at exactly the right moment in the trot stride while the outside hind leg is grounded and the outside foreleg is lifted. In sitting trot you can use your 'holding' aids of

above Leg-yielding in trot on a circle. Ketchup is showing good control of her outside shoulder. There is enough controlled bend for the size of the circle without her falling to the outside, and good engagement of the inside hind leg under the body mass.

right Leg-yield ridden along the track. Superficially, this leg-yield looks like a shoulder-in but it lacks bend through the body and lacks the collection required by shoulder-in.

the seat to maintain a steady rhythm. Your abdominal muscles can also be toned a little more to help form a base of support for your cob.

Ridden leg-yielding exercises

Once the basic leg-yielding has been developed in walk and trot you can begin to use it within schooling movements.

One exercise that I think works quite well is to leg-yield from a small circle out to a larger circle both in walk and trot. I will ride onto a 10 or 12m circle in the centre of a 20m circle area (see diagram). I will then leg-yield from the smaller circle out towards the 20m circle line. What I should mention is that you need a little more bend when leg-yielding on the circles.

Another exercise is to leg-yield from the outside track, in towards the three-quarter line of the school. Once you have ridden through the corner you should change bend to the outside then leg-yield in towards the three-quarter line using your outside leg. Once the three-quarter line is reached you can use the outside bend to turn out back towards the quarter marker of the school (see diagram). This exercise is great because it uses the gymnastic qualities of the leg-yield with the suppling effect of changing bend in a way similar to the 3 or 5m loops in from the track.

And finally, my favourite exercise. I enjoy riding a three-loop serpentine, making each loop about 2 or 3m smaller than normal (i.e. full arena size) then, using the bend of the loop, leg-yielding out to where the loop would normally go, before then changing the bend for the next loop (see diagram). This continues for the next loop but, on the final loop, I don't change the bend but continue out onto the outside track.

Shoulder-in

In the form required for dressage competitions, shoulder-in is ridden with the horse's body at a mean angle of about 30 degrees to the direction of travel, and on 'three tracks' – that is to say, the outside hind moves on one track, the inside hind and outside fore on a second, and the inside fore on a third track. The tracking for early shoulder-in (described as shoulder-fore), is on two-and-a-half tracks. This is because the shoulders come in just slightly. Really supple horses, advanced in

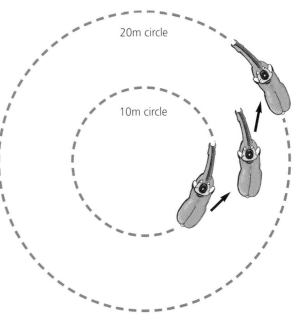

20m circle

10m circle

three-quarter line

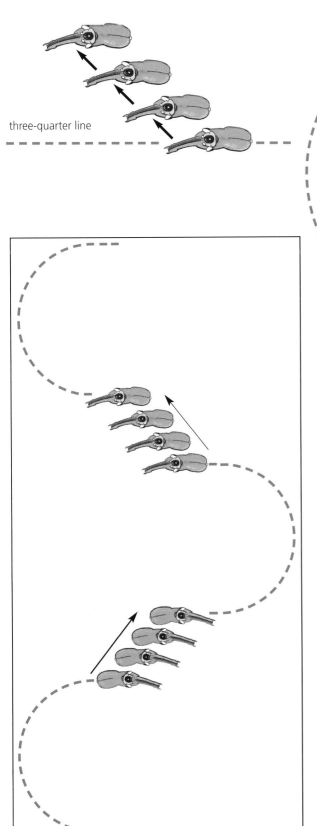

These are various leg-yielding exercises that I find useful. They add to the variety that we can give our cobs while schooling.

their training, are capable of performing shoulder-in on four tracks but, if this is attempted too early in training, the movement will lack bend and become a form of leg-yielding at an angle.

When introducing the exercise and at an early stage, we may have to make compromises in regard to both bend and angle. We cannot have the 'finished' shoulder-in when this movement is introduced because the cob will not be flexible enough or strong enough to produce it. Therefore, in the early stages of shoulder-in, the exercise really may resemble a leg-yield out on the track. However, developing this is part of the gymnasticizing process of the exercise and if we don't start developing the shoulder-in, we will never be able to develop the bend and strength necessary for an exceptional shoulder-in.

As mentioned earlier in the chapter (A Note from Experience) Ketchup really struggled to offer enough bend in the shoulder-in at first, and it took her some time to develop the suppleness and strength to offer a shoulder-in that maintains the angle, the rhythm, the quality that the Germans refer to as *losgelassenheit* (absence of tension) and, of course, the bend. However, once your cob reaches this more developed stage you will find that his angle will be maintained by the angle held in your own body, while your inside leg acts less to drive your cob sideways but rather asks for bend. At this stage your outside rein also becomes less necessary and can soften somewhat. This allows much more freedom and this is where the expressive trot stride and elevation of the forehand come from.

So, let's see how to go about introducing and developing this valuable exercise.

Introducing shoulder-in at walk

Of course, we only begin shoulder-in at walk. Only when the early shoulder-in is becoming established in walk can it really be developed in the trot. So let's start by describing the aiding and the riding of the early shoulder-in. The aids are broadly similar to the aids for leg-yielding but one major difference is that the inside leg is at the girth rather than behind it as in the leg-yield. I will always ride the first shoulder-in on the rein that the cob finds easier in-hand. I sit squarely in the saddle on the short side of the school. I then begin to ask for 'extra' inside bend and also for a little extra contact on the outside rein by using more inside leg with the swing of the cob's belly while 'holding' a little more with my seat and my abdominals. If need be I will ride a 10m circle in the corner to help set up the bend and give time for the preparation for the shoulder-in, but to be honest I don't always find this necessary, and often just use the bend developed for the corner to start the shoulder-in.

So, once I have finished the circle (if ridden) or am coming through the corner, I continue as though on the circle line until the cob's shoulders come in off the track. Once in this position, I increase the pressure of the inside leg on the girth in time with the swing of the cob's belly while 'blocking' the forward movement with my seat and, if need be, with a soft feel on the outside rein. (When I say blocking the forward movement, I don't mean discouraging a 'forward' impulse, but counteracting the cob's instinct to continue to move onto a circle or a diagonal line across the school, and redirecting him into moving along the track, with an inside bend.) This is achieved by my inside leg pushing him a little more along the track. An important point about setting up for the shoulder-in is that in positioning the cob correctly, you will find that your own body (in particular, your shoulders and hips) has turned a little more towards the centre of the school. This doesn't require any overt twisting of your body; it should be the case that, as you turn your cob to bring his shoulders inward, your own shoulders follow his. Basically, you allow your cob to place you. Once the cob is positioned to start the movement, the outside rein helps to prevent him from bringing his shoulders back to the track and losing his angle. (This should be achieved by keeping your outside rein low and in contact with the shoulder/withers area and vibrating against that area. Don't pull back or make your outside rein too tight, but feel as if you are nudging the shoulders over to the inside.) Your inside leg needs to work with the swing of the cob's belly and this allows your outside hip to advance at the same moment, thus taking your weight a little to the outside into the direction that you are asking the cob to travel. Stay square in the saddle, make sure that you do not collapse on either side, and remember that this is a collected movement in its finished form and, of course, an important exercise in developing collection, so make yourself proud and light. This exercise should, of course, be ridden on both

Shoulder-in on the right rein, showing good bend throughout the length of Ben's body.

reins. (In fact, while it is expedient to introduce it on the easier rein, it perhaps has greater gymnastic benefit when ridden on the more difficult rein, because it not only gives the rider more control over the bend and position, but also develops that weaker hind leg gymnastically.)

Shoulder-in at trot

The trot shoulder-in is ridden sitting and the aiding and use of the seat are exactly the same as for walk. The swing of the cob's belly allows you to sit into the direction of the movement by advancing your outside hip while using your inside leg. What I would emphasize in trot is the need to keep your cob from moving too fast; keep it slow (but active) and keep it soft.

In trot, it is often easier to collapse in your waist line so keep this in mind. To correct a shoulder-in without angle, turn away and start again. Have a feeling that you are exaggerating the angle at the start if need be; this is often necessary because riders often 'under-ride' the transition into the shoulder-in and thereby leave the cob's shoulders on the track. You can also use the whip on the inside at the same time as you use your leg. This can be particularly effective if you have started the shoulder-in in-hand, because your cob will understand these more established aids more readily than the 'new' ridden shoulder-in aids. Remember, however, that your whip aids need be no more than a stroke or a slight flick. Use the aids lightly and softly and your cob will develop lightly and softly; if you start with heavy aids you will end up having to ride much more heavily throughout.

The role of lateral work in developing the canter

As mentioned earlier, many aspects of schooling are complementary; what follows in this section is not necessarily about lateral work in canter – but about how the canter can be developed into a more 'uphill', balanced gait, once the early lateral work in walk and trot has given your cob more suppleness and the beginnings of collection. One point I would emphasize is don't maintain the canter for too long. It is always better from a schooling point of view to make a downward transition from a good canter than to have to make a transition once the canter had deteriorated. Also, it is the transitions that make the improvements, not the maintaining of the canter for longer periods,

Improving trot to canter

If you have followed the strategies mentioned for introducing canter in Chapter 4, you will have introduced canter in the school by working on a 20m circle. Now, riding at one end of the school in working trot, I advise starting by asking for clean transitions to canter just as you leave the track on the open side of the circle, maintaining the canter while riding round the open side of the circle, then asking for a downward transition when arriving back on the track. The trot phase can be used to rebalance the cob and this exercise can be maintained for six or seven canter transitions before changing the rein. At this stage, start asking your cob to maintain softness and a more rounded carriage in the canter strides, especially in the transition phase. Once this can be maintained for the six or seven strides, the canter can be extended to three-quarters of a circle, then a little way along the long side of the school. When you are ready to begin riding along the outside track, try asking for a little more softness to the inside as this often helps to maintain the outline and keep your cob a little straighter.

Improving walk to canter

Now that the early lateral work is really engaging and sharpening up the walk, this means that the walk to canter transitions should be on the road to perfection almost by default. What I often do at this stage is ride some leg-yielding and shoulder-in strides in walk before asking for the canter. These exercises help so much because, by their nature, they are actively engaging the inside hind leg under and across the body mass of the cob and, in canter, it is the inside hind leg that carries the forehand. So, for example, from the centre line in walk I will leg-yield out towards the quarter-marker then, as I arrive at the track before the corner, I ask for the canter and maintain it for six or seven strides before making a downward transition. If you try this you will find that your cob will lighten in the transitions up to the canter and he will feel lighter in the canter as a result. Ride this exercise for seven or eight transitions before changing the rein. If at any point your cob doesn't give you the requested transitions to canter, go back to the previous exercise to freshen up the canter transitions before re-introducing the lateral work to lighten and engage the transitions further.

The development of the walk to canter showing an increase in engagement and 'uphill' carriage. On the left Roxy is showing her first successful walk to canter transition, while on the right, Ketchup is showing what kind of transition Roxy is likely to give following many of these exercises.

Having schooled Lucky through a number of these exercises, her stride is really developing the spring necessary to maintain a more advanced way of going. Doesn't Lucky look fabulous?

Starting counter-canter

Once your cob can canter a little way while maintaining the bascule and spring, you can start to develop the counter-canter. This develops balance, straightness and the rider's ability to control the cob's shoulders at the canter. The most basic counter-canter exercise is to start riding in true canter, maintaining that lead in canter but riding 3 or 5m loops in from the track. When teaching this, I don't ask riders to change bend, as one does in trot, but I do ask that they don't exaggerate the bend over the leading leg. The canter seat doesn't change at all, but what I find is that the outside rein begins to play greater importance in maintaining straightness in the cob's shoulder. However, although your seat doesn't change as such, it does, as always, need to follow in the direction of the canter lead, so you can have a feeling of your body, seat and weight aids 'taking' your cob around the counter-canter part when he is on the 'wrong' lead. As you are on the loop, keep your outside leg back to help maintain the stride and use the outside rein in vibration to help the straightness as you are turning on the loop.

Once balance can be maintained on a 3m and then 5m loop in from the track, you can begin riding a 15m half-circle before riding back towards the midpoint marker at either E or B and changing the rein. First of all ask for two or three strides of counter-canter on the opposite long side of the school, then gradually you can ride through the first

Roxy in early counter-canter showing a balanced, relaxed stride. Caroline is well placed to help Roxy at any moment.

corner and, when balance can be maintained, you can canter through the second corner on the short side. Remember to keep riding into the direction of the canter stride and use your upper body and outside rein to bring your cob around the two corners of the short side of the school.

Counter-canter often gives riders their first feelings of true control and real collection in the canter. I love the feeling of counter-canter on Ketchup. It really feels like riding on the crest of the wave; like riding on air. This exercise really helped me develop control of Ketchup's canter stride and the counter-canter has really helped to develop some of her medium strides both at the trot and the canter – it is an excellent exercise that really is undervalued in the riding world.

Long and low stretching work in trot

As we have seen in The Role of Lateral Work in Developing the Canter, much schooling work is complementary. The relationship between the subject matter of this heading and lateral work is that, as mentioned, lateral work is one of the foundation stones of developing collection. At this stage, when early collection is being developed, long and low stretching in the trot should be introduced. At regular intervals throughout all collected work from now right through to advanced movements such as piaffe, you will need to allow your cob to stretch his

Long and low in trot with flexion at the poll. I don't generally want any more stretch than this in trot as, if any lower, it would put a cob very much on the forehand and would defeat the object of the stretching exercises.

topline forward and down as we discussed in respect of walk in Chapter 4. Never allow him to curl back behind the vertical, as this encourages him to 'hide away' from the bit and makes him less likely to seek a contact. In rising trot, ask for softness in your hands, then lower you hands on either side of his neck. Once he is soft, allow your hands a little forward with opening fingers, then ask again for a little more flexion before allowing with the reins a little more. Each time, feed the reins through your fingers a little at a time until your cob's poll is about level with or below his withers. Your body may incline a little more forward in the sitting phase, taking even more weight onto your thighs and knees so that you don't disturb your cob's back as he tries to round and lift it. Your legs keep asking his hind legs to swing and carry without speeding up nor slowing down.

CHAPTER SEVEN

Developing Engagement, Expression and Cadence

More advanced shoulder-in

The further into you cob's education you travel, the more important shoulder-in becomes. I am adamant that, in all of my schooling sessions and in the lessons that I teach, shoulder-in forms a vital component. The more you school your cob in the shoulder-in, the more important the bend becomes. In the previous chapter I made the point that, in the early days, the shoulder-in really resembles the leg-yield, that is, the cob moves laterally away from your inside leg but doesn't bend sufficiently throughout his body to engage the inside hind leg forward and under his body. Never forget, in your schooling of the shoulder-in, that the 'end product' should have a high degree of bend. The more correct bend your cob has throughout his body, the more engagement, collection and therefore expression will be developed. As your cob develops the strength required to deliver this type of shoulder-in, you will find that he puts himself into self-carriage much more readily; because of the increased bend he will lighten off the inside rein and carry himself with less intervention from you. He will maintain a light contact on the outside rein and you will notice that he will carry his shoulders to the inside without you having to push them there with the increased vibrations on the outside rein. Your cob will feel more as though he is curling around your inside leg rather than moving away from it. When he is at this stage you will feel a wonderful rhythm and wave of energy

Views of shoulder-in.

coming over your cob's back. Although both his shoulders will feel very light, you will notice much more expression and lightness in his outside shoulder.

I should reiterate here that these qualities are developments from the early shoulder-in and it takes consistent, well thought out school-ing to produce them. Rather than asking simply for sideways movement, your inside leg asks forward of the girth for bend with the swing of the belly. Just as you are doing this, your outside hip and seat bone are being pushed up and forward, advancing the movement down the track. This helps you to position your shoulders to the inside above your hips, but only as much as your cob has brought his shoulders to the inside. What you will find is, when your cob gets to this stage, you will merely need to think 'shoulder-in' and you will be away; it will feel as though he puts himself 'on the aids' for shoulder-in and the sensation will be magnificent. When Ketchup got to the stage of responding to such light aids in the shoulder-in all of her work improved in rhythm,

Ketchup showing her shoulder-in on the left rein.

Shoulder-in, rear view.

Shoulder-in, front view.

cadence and engagement. She came so light in my hands and she felt so 'up' and light in her forehand that I could hardly believe it. It is difficult to describe, but the moment you have got it you will know, and I can guarantee you will never forget it. It was enough to have the hairs on the back of my neck stand up.

In addition to the long sides of the school, shoulder-in can be performed on the short sides, on any straight lines, and also on circles, where the displacement of the shoulders to the inside is merely a continuation and exaggeration of the bend for the circle line. At an appropriate stage, shoulder-in can also be ridden in canter – see Chapter 8.

Travers and renvers

Travers and renvers are mirror images of each other. For example, in essence travers on the right rein with the bend to the right and the hips displaced further to the right, if performed on the left rein, would be a renvers! Confusing, isn't it? So let's separate the travers and the renvers.

Travers

In travers, the cob moves along the track with his head to the wall and his quarters to the inside. The bend is to the inside of the school. The tracking for early travers is described as three tracks, whereby the outside foreleg holds a track of its own. The inside foreleg and the outside hind leg form the second track while the inside hind leg follows a track all its own. More advanced travers can be performed on four tracks but the distances between the second and third tracks (inside foreleg and outside hind leg) need to be fairly close (some authorities call this three-and-a-half tracks as a result). If the distance between the second and third tracks becomes too great, then forwardness and balance will be compromised

In travers on the right rein, the cob will be bent to the right; his shoulders will remain on the track and the quarters will be brought further to the right onto an inner track, directed there by the rider's outside (left) leg. I only ever teach travers and subsequently renvers once the basic shoulder-in has been developed. The aids for travers are as much in the rider's seat as they are in the rider's legs. Again, using the right rein as an example, you will advance your inside (right) hip

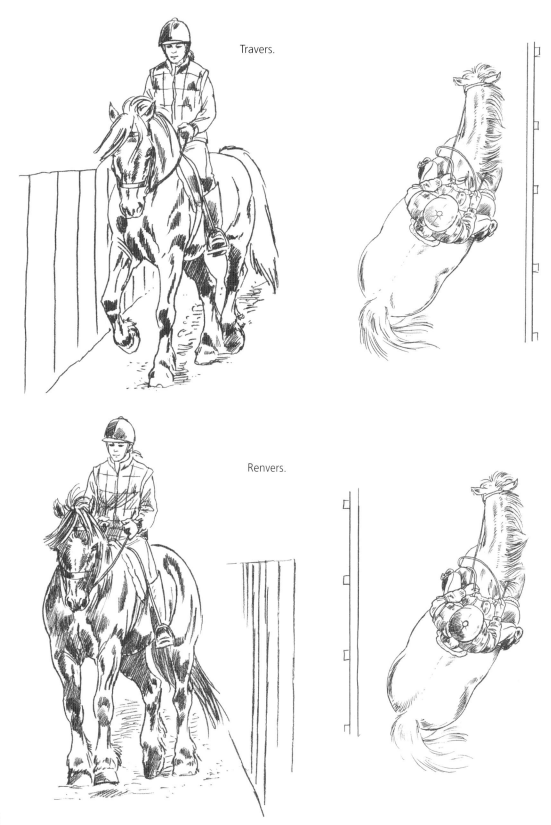

Travers.

Renvers.

more forward; this allows your outside hip and seat bone to slip a little more backwards in the saddle. This, in turn, positions your legs exactly where you need them to be – inside leg forward at the girth, and outside leg back behind the girth. As with shoulder-in, the outside leg acts in time with the swing of the cob's belly, allowing your outside leg aid to coincide with the action of the cob's outside hind leg as well as co-ordinating with the advancement of your inside hip and seat bone. The outside (left) rein is low and close to the withers, stopping the shoulder from jack-knifing out; the inside rein is slightly higher than the outside rein and is 'stacked' near the outside rein (by 'stacked' I mean that, in addition to being the higher rein, the inside rein is brought more towards your centre line so that it is almost on top of the outside rein). The inside rein asks for flexion to the inside – although, as in the shoulder-in, you will feel after a while that you can 'give that rein away', because the cob carries himself so much more.

As with shoulder-in, I introduce travers in walk, to allow the cob more time to understand what is required, and I also expect that it will take some time to produce the finished form.

I always teach travers out of a corner of the school. For example, on the right rein, just before coming out of the corner of the short side onto the long side, I make sure the walk is slow but diligent to the leg aids. I push my inside seat bone forward and raise my inside rein to flex the cob's nose to the inside then, with the swing of his belly, I pulse my outside leg to push the quarters to the inside. The moment the cob has brought the quarters to the inside, I reward well. At this stage don't be surprised if your cob drops the correct bend. Just make another transition into travers in the next corner and you will find that, through time, bend will develop, especially if you concentrate on the bend before the transition into travers. The more transitions you make into and out of travers, the better your travers will become. (Please remember that all exercises described as here on the right must be developed on the left rein also.)

At first the development of travers will follow a similar pattern to the shoulder-in, that is your cob will sidestep in a leg-yield type movement and it will be your job to introduce more and more bend throughout his body. You will soon begin to feel that your cob's shoulders will stay parallel to the fence and that the hindquarters will come in as a result of the bend, rather than having a body that is merely sidestepping along the wall of the school. Through time, enough bend will be developed to bring your cob from a three-track travers into a more advanced four-track one. Please remember that in the initial stages of teaching the travers, your cob will may appear to be on four tracks but it won't be as gymnastic an exercise because he won't have sufficient bend through the body.

Travers can be performed on the long sides of the school, on the short sides, on any straight lines, as well as on circles in the school, where the displacement of the quarters is merely a continuation of the bend for the circle line.

Renvers

As mentioned, renvers is a mirror image of travers but depends very much on the positioning of the cob in relation to the track and in which direction the bend is. Basically, travers has both the bend and the displacement of the quarters to the inside, into the middle of the school. Renvers, on the other hand, has both the bend and the quarters positioned to the outside of the school. (Your cob will have his shoulders displaced to the inside, while bend, and quarters will be to the outside.) I don't recommend riding renvers until you can ride travers successfully, because the nature of renvers means that at some point you either need to change the bend of your cob before displacing the quarters, or you have to assume a shoulder-in position then change the bend to the outside. This two-phase action requires more subtlety than either shoulder-in or travers and, as a result, many riders find this movement much more difficult.

The aids for renvers are essentially the same as for travers but reversed so, rather than positioning your seat to the inside, you position it to the outside of the school. Your inside leg (inside to the school, but which becomes the leg to the outside of the bend) is behind the girth and works with the swing of your cob's belly to push the quarters to the outside of the school. The inside rein (again inside to the school but outside to the bend) is low and vibrating against the neck, stopping the shoulders from falling too far to the inside of the school. The outside rein (inside to the bend) is held high, 'stacked' slightly above the inside rein (outside to the bend), flexing your cob to the outside of the school. I tend to ride on an inner track so that, when I ask the quarters to move to the outside of the school, they have room to do so. If you don't, you would just be pushing the quarters more and more into the fence.

As with the shoulder-in, at an early stage I just ride travers and renvers in walk and trot until the true bend is established and the cob maintains impulsion, rhythm and correct carriage. Then and only then can they be practised in canter. More important, however, I think is their use in combination with one another in walk and trot, as it is the transitions into and out of these movements that will build the flexibility and suppleness in your cob (more so, in fact, than the duration for which one particular movement is held). Once the shoulder-in, travers and renvers are fully developed, with good quality bend, these will be the key to developing expression and cadence in the basic gaits of walk and trot and will also help indirectly to develop an even lighter 'uphill' canter.

The half-pass

Once the travers and renvers have been established, it will be possible to use these exercises to develop the half-pass. Half-pass is a variation of travers, which is performed along a diagonal instead of along the wall. The horse stays more or less parallel to the long sides of the school but with some bend into the direction of the movement and the forehand slightly in front of ('leading') the hindquarters.

There are a number of ways of starting the half-pass, depending on whether it is the rider or the cob being taught – of course, it is much harder teaching both at the same time. So far as the rider is concerned, because the half-pass is ridden across the school rather than along a wall, I ask less experienced riders to imagine that there is a fence on a diagonal between say between K and M: in fact I sometimes give them ground-poles along this line, to follow. The aids for half-pass are, more or less, the same as for travers and are as much in the rider's seat as they are in the rider's legs. For example, on the right rein, you advance your inside hip more forward; this allows your outside hip and seat bone to slip a little more backwards in the saddle. This positions your legs exactly where you need them to be: inside leg forward at the girth, and your outside back behind the girth. The outside leg again acts with the swing of the cob's belly and this allows your outside leg aid to coincide *right* A nice view of half-pass on the diagonal line. This really does show the relationship between half-pass and travers. Ketchup is showing good bend into the direction in which she is moving.

far right A view of half-pass showing Ketchup's forehand clearly in front of the quarters. Her lateral steps are excellent and bend is good.

with the action of the outside hind leg as well as assisting the advancement of your hip and seat bone on the inside. The outside rein is low and close to the withers, stopping the shoulder from jack-knifing out; the inside rein is slightly higher than the outside rein and is 'stacked' (as explained earlier) near the outside rein. The inside rein asks for flexion to the inside although, as with shoulder-in, you will feel after a while that you can 'give that rein away', because the cob carries himself so much more.

When teaching half-pass to my cobs I always start in walk and always position them in shoulder-in for a few steps first. I do this to help the cob advance his shoulders first. (It is acceptable for the shoulders to be clearly in advance of the quarters in the early phases, and for the shoulders to be just marginally in front of the quarters in a finished half-pass. The quarters should never lead!) Then, for a few strides, I advance my inside hip, place my outside leg back behind the girth and use the leg in a pulsing action in time with the swing of the cob's belly. When teaching your cob, as he moves laterally into a half-pass, stop the aids and reward him lavishly. Remember, if he knows what you want, he is more likely to do what you ask. Initially ask only for one or two steps before rewarding him or moving back to shoulder-in. Then, before long, you will be able to ride an exercise of shoulder-in five strides, half-pass five strides. Use the shoulder-in periods to re-establish bend and rhythm before returning to half-pass. Once you are at the stage of riding this exercise for more than a few strides you can ride down the centre line and half-pass from the centre line back to the track at H or F. In this early stage, half-pass also can be performed from the quarter markers of the school to the centre line, or on any short diagonal line interspersed by either shoulder-in, circles or straight lines to re-establish rhythm, impulsion or bend. However, don't expect your cob to give you a half-pass across the whole of the long diagonal of the school at this stage; he needs great suppleness and collection to achieve this correctly, so take things slowly and don't push him or yourself too far, too quickly.

Walk pirouette

The walk pirouette is a movement in which the cob moves his fore-hand around his quarters, maintaining a walk rhythm. His quarters step around a very small circle and in a good pirouette the inside hind leg steps up and down in the correct rhythm more or less on the same spot, while the forehand moves around the quarters on a larger circle. The bend is in the direction that the pirouette is moving and although a full pirouette (through 360 degrees) is possible, a half-pirouette is more commonly seen.

I always develop the walk pirouette out of travers in walk on a circle. The circle line is gradually made smaller and smaller. At this stage, asking the cob to keep his quarters on the spot could lead to a spin, rather than a pirouette, so I keep the circle lines about 8–10m, holding the bend to the inside then asking the quarters to come in. Once the cob can hold this without losing his rhythm, then it is time to ask his quarters to come a little more to the inside for a stride or two before giving him the all-important reward.

Having explained the relationship with travers, I should add that the aids for the pirouette are almost identical to those for travers, except that the forward motion is denied a little and the outside rein asks a little more on the shoulder to push the outside shoulder round the pirouette line. So, from say, a 10m circle in walk on the right rein, the procedure is as follows. Start spiralling in towards a smaller (8m) circle.

Three pictures of moments in a walk pirouette to the right.

Ask for increased flexion to the right using a raised and 'stacked' inside (right) rein. Lower the outside (left) rein against the outside shoulder and use both your toned body and your vibrating outside rein to slow the walk down a little. Then ask the quarters to come in a little, again, as always, with the swing of the cob's belly. At this point put a little more pressure on the outside shoulder with the outside rein to encourage your cob to move into the direction of the pirouette. After a few successful steps, stop and reward. Gradually you can encourage these circles to be made smaller and smaller. When the pirouette circles are small enough for the hind legs to step more or less on the spot, you must be careful that the hind legs still step in the walk rhythm (hind legs that stand still in a pirouette are incorrect) and at this point work on the larger circles should resume: don't overdo the actual pirouettes; allow your cob to move more freely forward in between efforts.

Eventually you will be able to ask your cob for a pirouette from a walk on a straight line, from a shoulder-in on a straight line, or from walk on any circle line, all by merely changing your walk aids to the above-mentioned pirouette aids. Walk pirouette is a real 'collected' walk movement and, as a result of its schooling, your cob will develop more

expression in his walk and his strides will appear more 'cat-like'; as his quarters take more weight, his shoulders are able to elevate very much as a result.

Another three pictures showing moments in a walk pirouette, this time to the left.

Lateral work on a circle to develop expression in walk and trot

Once you are at the stage where your cob is established in shoulder-in, travers, renvers and walk pirouettes, you can use these exercises to develop much more expression and cadence in the walk and trot strides. The exercises used in combination also help to develop softness in outline, a much more consolidated absolute rhythm and, more than anything, a certain cadence and expression of stride that is the hall-mark of true collection. I will not discuss the aiding here as all of the aiding has been mentioned previously; however, what I will list is a variety of exercises that I use to help to develop these qualities.

All the while I am doing these exercises I am very diligent to ensure that the rhythm is maintained, that the cob maintains impulsion without rushing and that he maintains a certain softness in his mouth and in his outline. These points can often be achieved just by slowing the whole thing down.

One thing I often do is ride shoulder-in and travers alternately both in walk and trot on a 20m circle. Occasionally I will ask for a little more sideways movement and a little more angle in each of the shoulder-in and travers phases. After a while I will also introduce a change of bend without a change of rein to ride some renvers on the circle. Interspersed in all of this, there will be regular if not frequent changes of rein, transitions between walk and trot, walk pirouettes and of course straight (not lateral) work on circles, loops and serpentines.

You can also ride lateral exercises on a constant figure of eight (two conjoined 20m circles). For instance, shoulder-in could be ridden on the first circle of the figure of eight, followed by renvers after the change of rein on the second circle. Or you could ride travers on the first circle of the figure of eight then counter shoulder-in on the second circle. (Counter shoulder-in is basically shoulder-in to the outside, with bend and shoulders all positioned to the outside.) In both of these exercises you don't need to change bend when you change the rein; you merely change the displacement of the quarters or shoulders to suit the exercise required. You can then move on to exercises where your cob could change bend on each change of rein, for example from shoulder-in on one rein, to travers on the other, or renvers on one rein to counter shoulder-in on the other....

What I want to stress here is that you to take it all slowly; slow your cob down, and then gradually you can ask for a few 'exaggerated' strides – i.e. with more bend, more angle, and more sweep.

By going through these combined lateral exercises with Ketchup, I really found that all of her straightforward lateral work improved in bend and rhythm. She was able to give the true bend in the shoulder-in that gave me my first real glimpses of her self-carriage and collection. She began to give real sweeping strides in her half-passes without compromising her rhythm or impulsion. And, in all of her work, these exercises gave so much more suppleness and real pliability. Her transitions, her rhythm, engagement, responsiveness as well as forwardness all improved immeasurably as a result of this set of exercises. Done properly, the harder work really improves the easier work.

Introducing half-steps of piaffe

Once the lateral work is becoming more established, I always introduce half-steps of piaffe because this is an exercise which needs establishing slowly towards its finished form, and quite often a cob will need the collected feel from the half-steps of piaffe to help in the other exercises such as the lateral work mentioned above. Don't introduce this work until the lateral work is becoming established in walk and trot however, and don't run before you can walk – or should I say don't dance before you can step. For this work you will need the rein-back and so you can start schooling for this quite early on once the basic work is established.

Half-steps of piaffe. The steps are slower, less expressive and less engaged than in the full piaffe.

The rein-back

The aids for the rein-back are more about feel than they are about being specific with what you do here, there or elsewhere. The rider's basic posture is for you to take more weight down the front of your legs, and to lean your upper body a little forward in front of the vertical. What this does is to 'close the front door' and 'open the back door' weight-wise. Your legs swing a little way back behind the girth and apply a little pressure to instigate the first rein-back stride. Your hands maintain the flexed soft outline, and 'catch' any forward movement. Your hands do not make the cob step back! They must stay soft, as only a soft horse can step back into a correct rein-back. Of course, when you first teach rein-back you will need to halt on the outside track of the school. The fence will help to keep him straight. Adjust your body, apply the aids as described and don't allow your cob to move forwards. (Although you don't want to pull your cob back, you will need to catch any forward inclination in your hands if necessary.) The moment he steps back, stop your aids and reward. You will find quite quickly that your cob will step back from a slight pressure from your legs behind the girth and a slightly adjusted upper body position. You will also find that your hands only need to maintain softness in his mouth and neck, and soon your hands will play no more part in the rein-back than this.

The half-steps

So, using the rein-back and the trot you can begin to develop the piaffe, which is essentially a highly collected gymnastic trot on the spot. The piaffe can seen as the midpoint between a diagonal movement backwards (the rein-back) and a diagonal movement forwards (the trot). Of course, the early piaffe should not sit too much on the spot as this can cramp the hind legs (which will not have developed sufficient strength at this stage), but should move just a little forwards with each step. (At the highest level of competition, piaffe is allowed to move 1m forwards over twelve steps, but at this very early stage, forward movement in piaffe-type steps should not be inhibited.)

To begin teaching the piaffe, I tend to ride very short bursts of collected trot followed by halt then rein-back. Out of the rein-back I ride forwards into the collected trot. Gradually, and I mean *very* gradually, I begin to keep the trot a little more on the spot – that is, I shorten the steps of the collected trot out of the rein-back by toning my upper body slightly and by keeping my body from 'letting go' into a bigger trot. My lower legs stay back a little and my body stays upright. Gradually, I ask for a couple of trot steps to 'bounce' more on the spot, before allowing the trot out to a bigger collected or even working trot again.

When you begin this schooling, only work on this for a few minutes before returning to more forward work, as it is very taxing. Your hands throughout this exercise maintain softness in your cob's mouth and only guard against too much forward movement as in the rein-back; it is your body that really stops too much forward movement coming through. These few bounce steps that move a little forward are the steps that can be built up to a piaffe, moving forward only very slightly.

This same exercise can be mirrored in-hand. Put your cob in a cavesson, and practise rein-back to trot transitions, always maintaining softness, and, if your cob gets too strong, return to rein-back-walk-halt transitions. Again, you can gradually prevent the trot phases from going too far forward and as a result it will appear that you cob will 'bounce' a little more on the spot. In-hand as when ridden, the moment your cob gives you these bounces, stop and praise him. Maintain these short – and I mean very short phases (two or three strides, no more!) – for a while, as it is more important to develop your aiding, your cob's strength and the rhythm over a longer period, than it is to develop a lengthy sequence of piaffe steps held on the spot.

Once he will give you these bounce strides out of rein-back, both in-hand and ridden, you can begin to ride these movements with more of a feeling of shoulder-in to help give more elevation to the forehand. (This can also be used to correct a piaffe that is crooked.) It is at this time that you can ask for a couple of extra steps in the piaffe – going up to five or maybe six. If your cob begins to flag a little in his half-steps, make a vigorous transition to a more forward trot for a dozen or so strides before asking again for the piaffe steps. Don't be tempted to use stronger leg aids or to keep pushing. (When I say more forward and energetic I never mean harsh, strong or sharp – just positive and assertive smooth riding). The piaffe is the proof of impulsion; energy can't be put in whilst in the piaffe, but it can be corrected by riding more energetic transitions into and out of it. This sequence should be developed over months and months, not days or weeks. It takes years to develop a great piaffe. The slower and steadier you take it at this early stage, the better the foundations laid for a consistent and gymnastic piaffe in the future.

You will find that once work in piaffe half-steps has commenced, all of your cob's work will reflect this extra engagement. The work with the combined lateral exercises mentioned earlier will be so much more expressive; the canter will be much lighter and your cob will become softer and higher in his outline and his self-carriage will improve no end.

Little did I know that introducing piaffe to Ketchup would lead me down such an exciting path! I had been told that Ketchup was the wrong raw material if I was serious about dressage, and I suppose by introducing piaffe there was an air of wanting to prove 'them' wrong – I wanted to prove that dressage was a series of exercises designed to improve any horse, whether a pony, a Warmblood, a Thoroughbred or 'even' a cob. When we began, Ketchup's start in piaffe was just like a chicken scratching at the dirt. But slowly – it has been said by some teachers – her piaffe has developed into one that could now rival many horses in international competition! The piaffe has been Ketchup's key to engagement. As a result of developing her piaffe, Ketchup has established a very light, 'uphill' way of going which has really been a key to improving difficult exercises in canter. It has to be said that her piaffe comes second only to her ability in her lateral work at the trot.

Lengthening the stride

You will notice that I have left this rather later than most instructors and trainers would in their horses' education. I think there is a very good reason for this. Cobs are often built very much onto their forehand with big, heavy shoulders and, if rushed, all cobs tend to get heavy, ploughing onto the hands of their riders. Their hocks are very active, and if they haven't been taught to 'carry' a little before being asked to lengthen out their strides, cobs are more likely to run, flattening their stride and getting heavier on the hands as just mentioned.

Therefore, I always wait until the cobs I train can show full collection in walk and trot, and also are capable of some half-steps in piaffe, before I open them out into a more lengthened stride at medium trot or extended walk. (This does not mean, however, that I don't use long and low methods of stretching throughout schooling.) At first, I only ask for a few strides of either extended walk or medium trot, probably no more than five or six of each. The transitions into each are ridden progressively as this gradual transition means you can adjust your aids more gradually and helps to guard against the cob being thrown out of balance. (Please note that unless your cob is much more balanced in the canter than has been outlined so far, I would not advise ride any lengthened strides at canter – the canter may need much more work!)

Extended walk

Extended walk is always far easier to ride than any lengthened strides of trot or canter. All you need to do is to allow a certain amount of stretch in your cob's neck, without allowing him to come too low in his outline, and to increase your leg aids as described in Chapter 3 – that is, each leg pulsing on your cob's side with the swing of his belly. Guard against a quickening of his stride by maintaining tone through your body and by being deliberate with the rise and fall of your seat bones. Extended walk is merely a variation of walk on a long rein, but your cob will need to maintain a higher head-carriage while keeping the length of neck and stride that were established in the free walk on a long rein.

In the early days, extended walk looks more like free walk on a long rein.

Lengthened (medium) strides in trot

I always establish these step by step. Initially two strides then increasing until four or five can be achieved without a change of rhythm or balance. Once this is achieved, I merely allow the sequences to lengthen to seven, then eight, then more strides. I always come to the medium trot strides from exercises such as the combined lateral exercises described earlier or soon after the piaffe half-steps practice. This is because these exercises really build the flexion in the hindquarters

This rider has cleverly allowed her Dales pony to take his nose forward in the lengthened trot. The length of stride achieved is good. The rider has moved her legs a little forward to help.

necessary for the cob to lengthen his stride without pushing the extra stride length onto his forehand.

So, from the exercises mentioned, proceed in a collected trot (go rising trot in the early stages) maintaining that absolute 'tick-tock' rhythm. If your primary concern is the rhythm then you won't go far wrong. In this trot, start to feel as though you are slowing the rhythm down a touch. (I always think this because the medium trot should have exactly the same rhythm as the collected trot, but as we ride more forward for the lengthened strides we can often let the rhythm quicken – so remember rhythm first!) As you slow that rhythm, start to push with your legs on the girth or a little way in front of the girth with each stride as you sit. Remember only gradually ask for two or three strides then return to a more collected stride. Repeat the exercises mentioned earlier to bring your cob back onto his hocks, then repeat your request for a more open stride. Don't do too much as we don't want all of the work done in getting your cob off his forehand to be undone in a few moments in medium trot. You will hopefully feel that your cob pushes your pelvis further forward through the air as you rise to the trot; allow this but don't force it. Keep him soft but don't 'throw the reins at him', allowing all of the energy to gush out of the front door. Your reins in this instance are your valves; allow just enough to let the outline to

The last few steps of medium trot in competition. I have eased my shoulders forward so I can give Ketchup a scratch on her shoulders as a reward for a good attempt.

lower slightly and lengthen out a touch, but not so much that you can't adjust the feel if necessary. Begin to build more and more on these strides, always returning to piaffe half-steps or lateral work in between to bring him back onto his hocks. Remember rhythm first!

More transition work in canter

So far, your canter will be improving without much work on that gait itself, but purely as a result of the gymnastic benefits of the work in the lateral steps and the early piaffe. All these exercises will really sit your cob onto his hocks, which will be used to great advantage in the canter.

Transitions to canter can be made from any of the lateral steps mentioned so far, but I have to say that I really use only the leg-yield, the shoulder-in and the walk pirouette to prepare for the canter transitions. One of the most successful exercises that I have found with Ketchup is the shoulder-in, in walk up to canter. The ensuing canter is almost always soft in the hand, and is beautifully 'uphill'. The canter need be maintained for only six strides before a transition to trot and then walk before the whole thing is repeated. (You will also find with this exercise that your cob will soon be making transitions to walk in response to you using a slightly stronger seat aid and a greater tone held through your body.) This exercise can be developed into six strides of walk

While warming up for competition, I am using the transitions exercise to really engage Ketchup. On the left is her first canter and on the right is the canter achieved after a few transitions. It really works, doesn't it?

shoulder-in, six strides of canter, then from this, longer periods of canter can be developed while maintaining softness and rhythm. The shoulder-in gives softness and bend to the inside and a deeper flexion of the inside hock needed for a lighter canter. Going on from this exercise, counter-canter and bounce poles can be ridden to take advantage of the more 'together' canter strides.

The same pattern of exercises can be followed with the walk half-pirouette, though a change of bend will be necessary before the canter transition. (This is because I usually ride, for example, a walk pirouette to the left on the track, changing the rein through the pirouette, then change bend from left to right to commence right canter.)

Another variation of riding transitions into canter is the rein-back to canter. This really is a wonderful exercise for getting your cob to take more weight onto his hindquarters and for developing that 'uphill' quality that makes the canter so beautiful. In its advanced form, the cob will spring forwards into a well-balanced canter straight out of rein-back, but in this very early form I would recommend that you ask for a couple of strides of walk just before the canter transition. Only three or four steps of rein-back will be needed before you move your upper body back to vertical, allowing the walk to come out of the rein-back. Then allow your inside leg forward, outside leg back a little and ask for your canter after a couple of strides. After a while – a few weeks or months

∧ Dales pony showing a more advanced way of going in canter, with fantastic engagement and elevation. The rider is framing her mount well, too.

after first practising this exercise – you can reduce your intermediate walk steps until your cob can spring from rein-back steps into a well balanced canter. (As the transition to canter becomes more immediate, co-ordinating the timing of the aids to the positioning of the cob's legs becomes more crucial.)

Although Ketchup had previously shown some really great glimpses in the canter, it wasn't until we began to practise the rein-back to canter that the 'uphill' quality became much more evident. Once this exercise was established, Ketchup could maintain much longer sequences in the canter without losing the fragile balance. I think this exercise really helped her: it brought her poll up and helped to keep her nose just in front of the vertical, if not on it. The rein-back really rounded Ketchup's back and brought her hind legs under, into a more collected position, and all this without having to resort to pulling on the outside rein and kicking with the inside leg. Surely that is proof enough that this really does work, and is a pleasure to work through for both cob and rider!

It is only once this stage of work has been reached successfully that longer canter sequences can be practised, because it is only at this point that your cob will have sufficient engagement in his canter to maintain a good canter through all the figures that have been ridden so far in trot. These can include a transition into the canter, a series of

Photos showing Ketchup in the moment of the transition from rein-back into canter. Both are 'uphill' and engaged. The photo on the left shows more cadence of the stride while maintaining a more open poll. On the right, Ketchup is rounder, but has lost some of that cadence as a result.

circles varying in size from 20m down to 10m, then a loop in from the track in counter-canter or even a half-circle changing the rein, returning to the track in counter-canter. Build up to such work at first; try one circle, then one-and-a-half circles and go back to transition exercises if the rhythm and balance are lost.

....

CHAPTER EIGHT

Further Advancement in the Canter

Once your cob's balance is established in a much more 'uphill' carriage, lateral work will bring about more manoeuvrability, more bounce and engagement as well as collection in the canter. But before we discuss these lateral movements in canter I want to develop further an idea that I touched upon in the previous chapter – the balance that the rein-back to the canter has produced. Once the feeling of this 'uphill' balance has revealed itself, you can help by asking your cob to maintain it by asking him to raise his carriage and keep his poll up. However, I would emphasize the need to maintain softness while you raise his poll. It is no good just pulling his head higher and higher as you will inevitably hollow him and ultimately disengage him too much. So, from a rounded outline, simply raise your hands for a few moments while asking your cob to step up a little with your legs; guard against him speeding up by adding extra tone in your body and then, after a few moments, release your aids (especially your rein aids) but maintain your improved rhythm and tone through your body. This really works in all gaits – it can help, for example, after combined lateral movements to bring about that 'cat-like' quality in the collected walk and trot. In canter, it can help to maintain this feeling just before and into the lateral work in order to keep your cob from becoming too forward and falling onto his forehand.

Mister Mints showing a visibly shortened, cadenced canter. His outline is great and he is being framed by a particularly skilled and talented rider.

Lateral work in canter

Canter shoulder-in

This is achieved by asking for more bend in the canter stride. So, coming round the short side of the school, ask for more bend through your cob's whole body then, when arriving on the long side, think about bringing his shoulders in, in the same way as you would in walk or trot. Then, in rhythm with the canter stride, pulse your inside leg forward at the girth when your cob is at the lowest phase of the canter stride. Have a feeling that, not only are you bending him around that inside leg, but also that it is bringing his forehand up in every stride. The nature of canter shoulder-in really helps to stop a cob who is heavy on his forehand from ploughing down onto his rider's hands.

Although I generally practise canter shoulder-in on the long sides of the school, at times I also ride it on a 20m circle and when the cob is more advanced I ride it on the centre line – very difficult but very worthwhile.

Canter half-pass

The aids for this movement are really a continuation of the canter aids. From that really 'uphill' canter that we have been developing, I would recommend that you start teaching the canter half-pass from the long side. This is so that, when you get to the end of the school you don't have to change the rein; you can have a couple of attempts in the half-pass before then changing the rein to have a go on the other rein. So, coming out of the second corner of the short side, ask your cob to maintain the bend, keep your inside seat bone advanced forward and pulse your outside leg behind the girth in rhythm with the canter stride when your cob is at the lowest phase of the canter stride, as though you are 'scooping' him a little sideways. 'Stack' your inside hand a little higher to ask for flexion to the inside; your outside rein is low on your cob's withers, vibrating against the withers and pushing his shoulder over. The moment your cob's canter stride feels as though it bounds sideways, stop and reward him.

Canter half-pass to the right, showing good bend and form.

There will come a time when your cob will become so enthusiastic about his canter half-pass that you will have to stop him from using the increased momentum of the canter to throw himself more sideways. To remedy this, I ask for the canter half-pass then, the moment he stops 'sitting', I stop him, return to walk and start again, re-establishing the canter and asking again for the half-pass. If you follow this procedure you will soon find that your cob will be able to make mini-jumps sideways without losing balance or allowing the momentum to pull him sideways. Remember to keep your body upright; do not allow your upper body to collapse to either direction in an attempt to move your cob more sideways: your inside seat bone position is sufficient for this.

Once this basic work has been achieved you can start developing the canter half-pass from the centre line back to the track. When you do this, remember that you will either have to make a transition to trot once you reach the track, or you will have to ride round at least part of the bottom of the school in counter-canter. Both add increased challenge, but both are very worthwhile. I enjoy riding a variation of a figure of eight. I half-pass from the centre line back to the track, then maintain counter-canter round the bottom of the school before changing the rein again. This variation of the exercise really engages the cob and keeps him listening.

Canter travers

I only tend to use this exercise to develop the canter pirouette, because canter is probably the gait in which the cob is most likely to be crooked, and by practising travers one may inadvertently compound this problem. This work should only be started when the cob is established in canter shoulder-in as well as canter half-pass. When that time comes I always ride travers on a circle and never on straight lines because of the straightness issues mentioned above.

So, from the canter circle, start asking for a little more inside bend, then adopt the travers aids; push your inside seat bone a little more forward and pulse your outside leg behind the girth in rhythm with the canter stride when your cob is at the lowest phase of the canter stride, as though you were 'scooping' his quarters a little sideways and into the centre of the circle. 'Stack' your inside hand a little higher to ask for flexion to the inside; your outside rein is low on your cob's withers, helping to maintain the shoulders on the outer circle line; the reins and hand position also help to position the quarters to the inside. Maintain this for a couple of strides before rewarding. Don't build up to too many strides at this stage: five or six strides of travers on a circle will be more than adequate.

At first, stay on that 20m circle so that you are not overtaxing your cob. Only after a few months of practising this can you begin to make the circle smaller, down to 15m and then 12m. Any time that you feel your cob swing sideways as a result of the momentum, stop him and re-establish the canter from a balanced walk to canter transition. Later, when he is at the stage of developing the full pirouette, this is the exercise that will be mainly practised, because it is far less taxing than the

Rear view of canter travers. The image shows the collecting qualities of the movement.

pirouette itself and it is the exercise that riders use to correct faults in the fully collected canter pirouette.

Ketchup loves this work and it is the exercise that I use more regularly than the actual pirouette to keep her hind legs stepping in the rhythm of the canter.

Canter to walk and simple changes

Canter to walk

The canter to walk has been touched upon earlier but now we can spend a little more time developing it. I always do this later rather than sooner, as cobs tend to be very easy to tip onto their forehands and really do need this extra engagement to step forward into the walk from a collected canter without ploughing onto the rider's hands. If your cob hasn't offered a transition to walk as a result of the transition exercises worked on so far, don't force one by pulling on the reins, but begin to develop the direct transitions through more focused downward transitions.

Your cob should now be capable of good transitions from a quality canter to a rhythmical, controlled trot, and of course from a controlled trot to a walk. So, beginning in the canter, make a transition to the controlled trot, then count six trot strides before making a transition to walk. Reward all good transitions and reward generously the moment you get the walk. Then begin reducing the intermediate trot strides first from six to five and then, through time, these can be reduced to four, then three, then two and usually before you get to one trot stride, your cob will get the idea and will make a direct transition forwards to walk. I developed this method with Ketchup because although she would go from canter to walk she would hollow momentarily just as she stepped to walk. I knew she stayed round in canter to trot transitions and could maintain an absolute trot rhythm, and she could maintain softness in a transition from trot to walk. So I started the above-mentioned exercise to maintain softness. Once you have reached the stage when you are riding only two or three strides of trot between the canter and the walk you will need to make your aiding stronger in your seat, thighs and abdominals; this is usually enough to bring about the transition required. Remember, reward generously and your cob will get the idea!

Simple changes

A simple change of leg is basically where the horse canters on one lead, makes a transition to walk, then walks only a couple of strides before making a direct transition into canter on the other lead. These simple changes can be developed from the transitions to walk. In fact, once the canter to walk is established, the simple change really looks after itself.

First of all, make things easy for yourself and your cob. Make your transition say from canter right to walk. Give your cob time in the walk to settle and change bend to the left. Only when he is ready, ask for a direct transition to canter left. Gradually you can decrease the walk strides down to five or four, but don't rush to get to that stage; take your time and only move on when you and your cob are both ready.

For higher-level showing, simple changes will be necessary as they will give you the edge. A canter schooled to the level where a simple change is possible will be noticeably lighter than one that is not. So not only will it give you the edge in a showing ring with regard to canter quality but it will also give you the opportunity to show how manoeuvrable your cob really is. In showing, of course, your cob will not be marked on how clean the downward transition is in the same way as in the dressage arena but I do think it could be a key movement to school for improved results in showing.

Lengthened (medium) strides at canter

As with so many matters at this level, if your collection and engagement in the canter are good then medium strides in canter will take care of themselves. I ride the medium canter only as part of a sequence of other exercises, and for no more than three or four strides; we don't want to spoil that fragile balance that we have worked so hard to get.

My favourite sequences which help to develop the medium canter have already been mentioned. For example, ride canter half-pass from the centre line back to the track, then maintain counter-canter round the bottom of the school before changing the rein across the diagonal. When on the diagonal line, begin to increase pressure from both your legs, a little further forward again and, as always, in the canter rhythm. Allow the canter stride to open up by permitting the increased flexions in your lower back. But don't allow all of the energy to be 'thrown out the front door' by pushing with your seat. Your seat only moves as much as your cob lengthens. Soften slightly with your hands so your cob can match the length of his stride with the length in his neck, but not so much that all connection is lost. Remember, start with only two or three lengthened strides before collecting your cob ready for the looming corner. To help collect, have a feeling of riding shoulder-in into the corner and retard the forward movement with your seat, but use your leg aids so your cob doesn't break into trot. This exercise really sets up the medium canter by engaging your cob through the half-pass and the counter-canter and uses the corner after the medium strides to help to collect him again.

Another exercise that I really like is performed on the track. From canter shoulder-in on the track (only two or three strides) straighten your cob a little along the track, then open him out as described above for two or three strides before collecting and riding another two or three canter shoulder-in strides before the corner. This exercise ensures a good collected canter before and after the medium canter and also helps to straighten a crooked medium canter.

Ketchup really enjoys both of these exercises; they both set her up well for the medium canter and make sure that the lengthening really comes from deeper-set, flexing hind legs, not from the speed that can be associated with pushing horses more onward. Her shoulders are

A medium canter ridden in forward seat out in the fields. Look at the engagement of the hind leg during the medium strides.

Lynn Russell showing an expressive extended canter in the show ring. Lynn's position is framing and balancing the cob well. The length of outline and stride is great in this canter but for perfection I would like the poll to be the highest point and for the nose to be a little more forward.

always up and free as a result. Both exercises have really helped her downward transitions to a collected canter, but I have to say that it is the shoulder-in exercise that I prefer for that. The nature of the canter shoulder-in really stops Ketchup from bearing down onto her forehand in the transition from medium to collected canter by keeping her hind legs flexing and carrying the forehand.

With time, you can begin to ask for longer periods of medium canter, but always ride it as a part of a greater sequence that keeps your cob from ploughing onto his forehand and onto your hands.

When moving your cob forward in the show ring, you will have more room than in a dressage arena. The judge will look for a braver amount of acceleration into the showing 'gallop' and a clear transition back while in dressage, although a clear transition into the medium canter is required, rhythm needs to be maintained and any loss of harmony will be easily picked up by the dressage judge

Flying changes

As long as you have maintained and advanced your inside hip and seat bone in canter, and have a deep inside leg and an outside leg that maintains its position behind the girth in all your canter work, then you shouldn't have too much trouble getting your first flying change.

The aids for the flying change in canter are exactly those of a canter transition. However, if you are, for example, on the right leg, you need to adopt canter left position with your seat and the leg and rein aids. Change your aids the stride before you want the flying change, increase pressure from your new outside leg and, at the same time, advance your new inside seat bone a little more. This process was definitely enough for Ketchup to give her early flying changes, but if it is not so for your cob, increase the pressure from your new outside leg as you exaggerate your inside seat bone position, and at the same time give a little tap of the whip behind your new outside leg while toning your body in the new canter direction so that the aiding doesn't push your cob too far forwards. Remember to reward all early attempts. Riding flying changes is as individual as all horses, cobs and ponies are, so you are going to have to respond appropriately to what your cob gives you.

I tend to ride a flying change after a period of counter-canter because counter-canter can be taxing and the cob may offer a change more readily to 'get away' from the demands of the counter-canter. Some of my favourite places to ride flying changes are after a counter-canter loop, after canter half-pass when returning to the track and on the centre line while riding three-loop serpentines. Ketchup's all-time favourite is after riding a 10m half-circle to the centre line, then returning to the track in a tear shape. I can really feel her bubble with anticipation for the few strides before the change (and if I don't make the change I can feel her disappointment!). At the time of writing, Ketchup is still perfecting her flying changes and really needs to 'calm' herself over them because her anticipation can make her a little silly and headstrong! When she was introduced to flying changes I'm sure she thought she was a Lipizzaner, often leaping up in the air!

In showing, as well as dressage and jumping classes, the flying change can be a valuable exercise to add to your cob's repertoire.

....

CHAPTER NINE

The Culmination of Collection

The movements mentioned in this chapter are often thought of as the real hallmarks of dressage or classical riding. They truly are beautiful movements, but I must stress that they are no more classical or beautiful than the correctly balanced 20m circle in trot at Preliminary level. For without that correctly balanced circle at the beginning of a horse's education, he will never develop gymnastically to the point at which that he can offer classically correct piaffe, passage or pirouette steps. If the piaffe, passage or pirouette are developed without such foundations in place, only grotesque approximations will result as the horse won't have the balance, manoeuvrability, cadence or strength to cope with them. Damage will be the only result! What I am trying to say here is celebrate all of your achievements. A great trot with rhythm and balance is to be celebrated just as much as a piaffe! Without the trot, you will never get the piaffe, just as without the balanced, 'uphill' canter you will never get the pirouette.

Piaffe

If you have worked diligently on the piaffe half-steps mentioned in Chapter 7, your cob's piaffe should be coming along nicely, so now it is time to develop this work towards a more finished piaffe. Now you can start to hold the piaffe a little more on the spot for a stride or two. Begin to sit a little taller in the piaffe for up to five strides before allowing it

Two images of Ketchup in piaffe. Both are 'uphill' with good hind legs, but the one on the left shows less triangulation of the forelegs (where the leg creeps back under the body) and is thus more correct.

forward again, riding a feeling of shoulder-in in the piaffe to help keep the steps straight. You may wonder why an element of shoulder-in – an exercise with lateral bend – can help to maintain straightness. Quite often, your cob will try to alleviate the pressure put on his hindquarters in piaffe by pushing his shoulders to one side and his quarters to the other. The track, for example, can be an irresistible magnet for your cob's shoulders. If this is the case his quarters will swing in and therefore not engage under the body mass. An element of shoulder-in helps because you take control of the shoulders, keeping them where you need them, and this makes it easier for your cob to engage his hindquarters under his body mass.

You can begin to ask for piaffe on the centre line, across the middle of the school and, more importantly, out of walk and trot. You should no longer need to start from the rein-back; the aids and the feel for the piaffe should be much more established, allowing you 'pop up' into piaffe from walk, or to add a bit more collection to step into piaffe from the trot.

The most important aspect is to think of having your cob truly 'uphill'. As mentioned in the previous chapter, when describing the more advanced canter, you will need to maintain this balance by asking your cob to raise his carriage to keep his poll up. Remember to maintain softness while you raise his poll – and especially remember that you don't want to hollow your cob – the essence of the piaffe is to lower the quarters and round the back.

So, from a rounded outline, simply raise your hands for a few moments while asking him to step a little with your legs in the piaffe position. Guard against speeding up by adding that extra tone in

An expressive piaffe ridden in a shoulder-in position. Ketchup's poll is up and nose out slightly. Many might claim that this is hollow, but I would dispute that. No triangulation is shown here.

A rounder piaffe; many would prefer this way of going to that shown in the upper photo. Ketchup's hind legs are well under and her outline looks soft. But there is an element of triangulation showing in this piaffe, which is thus of a poorer quality than the one above.

your body; release your rein aids after a few seconds but maintain your improved rhythm and the tone through your body. This really works to keep the piaffe 'uphill' and stops your cob from taking too much weight onto his forehand, which manifests itself in triangulation of the forelegs. When viewed from the side, your cob's forelegs should look perpendicular to the ground. In a triangulating piaffe the forelegs look as though they creep back towards the hind legs. (One exception to this is if your cob stands naturally with his forelegs behind the vertical; in this case you wouldn't want him to piaffe with his forelegs at a greater angle than he stands at naturally.) Ketchup stands slightly back at the knee, so she tends to look a little like an elephant on a drum in piaffe, but as long as I concentrate on keeping her carriage up, I can prevent her from allowing her forelegs to creep back too far.

Passage

Passage is a very collected, stylized form of trot where the horse takes much shorter, higher steps in the trot while exaggerating the moment of suspension. In effect, he takes more 'deer-like prancing' type steps in the trot. Ketchup found the introduction to the passage very difficult. Whereas the piaffe entails a real carrying movement in the hind legs, the passage requires as much pushing as carrying, and it took a really long time for Ketchup to understand that we needed both qualities in passage, not just the push of the hocks or the flexion of the hindquarters! To convince her, I had to use a variety of different methods, but hopefully at the time of writing we are meeting in the middle with all of these techniques to produce a good passage worthy of an Advanced dressage competition.

Cobs will never passage with the training techniques used by many modern dressage riders. These people tend to train the passage by 'retarding' the forward impulsion in medium trot. If you do this with your cob you will produce a very heavy, stilted and unhappy cob. You will need to start weight training just to hold him up! My chosen path to training the passage is far, far softer.

Start in the piaffe and just as you are beginning to 'sit' the piaffe more on the spot, also start riding sequences of it more forward. You maintain that rounded back as well as the piaffe rhythm but increase your leg aids to ask your cob to go a little more forwards and just 'give'

Ketchup showing a fantastic 'airborne' passage.

enough with your body to allow these more forward steps without losing that rounded back or the piaffe rhythm. With some cobs, this may be enough to bring about a passage step. If it is, and you will know if it is by the increased vertical force, praise, praise and praise again. The step that your cob has just taken can be a daunting one! If, however, this aiding only brings about an opening of the piaffe step then you will need to convince him to raise the height of his foreleg action and then increase the upward push in each of his hocks within the stride, and this can be achieved by using the influence of the loftier strides of the Spanish walk.

Introducing Spanish walk to help with passage

The following sequence takes months to develop and perfect so please don't rush it! I always start by introducing the Spanish walk aids on the ground with in-hand work. Usually, only a cavesson is needed; all that is necessary at this stage is to tickle the cob either behind his knee or down on his fetlock until he responds by raising his leg. When he does this, reward him.

Continue with this until he responds to lighter and lighter aids; it is at this stage that you could 'take the steps for a walk'. Slow the walk down and just before he lifts say, his left foreleg, tickle it with the whip. If he responds by raising his leg higher within the walk rhythm, remember to reward again. Soon, you can ask each foreleg alternately on consecutive steps with the whip (you'll need to be quick!). If your cob gives two lofty strides in the walk, reward him. You can then build up the number of strides from here.

This work can be developed by progressing in a similar way ridden. Start by halting out on the track. Use your whip down on the shoulder, pointing towards the leg that you are intending your cob to lift. Tickle him either on the shoulder or down the leg and, if he responds, pat him and reward him well. When he will do this with both his forelegs from halt you can ride forward to the walk, keep it slow and ask, say, for the left leg to raise higher by tickling your cob down the shoulder and onto his leg as it is grounded. Remember to reward well if he responds as you hoped.

Rather than expecting the cob to raise alternate legs when ridden, I tend to ask the same leg to raise higher step after step before changing to the other leg. Only when your cob will lift each leg, stride after

Fantastic stepping in Spanish walk. Any Iberian horse would be proud of a Spanish walk like this: it really is Ketchup's party piece.

stride, should you then begin to ask him to raise both legs alternately. However, I have to say that many horses (including Ketchup) often offer the alternate lifting of legs without being asked. Ketchup 'just knew' and of course the moment she gave two consecutive lofty strides I rewarded lavishly! She has never looked back. (I have to add that I only taught Ketchup the Spanish walk to help develop the passage, but now that it has been developed I'm sure it has also improved all her other work by introducing more expression to her stride as well as cadence in her more collected work. Ketchup now uses the Spanish walk as her party piece, and I have to say that she can now do the Spanish walk as well as any horse of Iberian descent. Well, take a look at the expressive picture and decide for yourself. Fantastic, isn't she?)

Developing expression in the passage using the effects of Spanish walk.

Developing passage

Once you can request these lofty strides ridden in the walk, you can work on the piaffe that moves forward. In this movement, you can ask for a loftier stride of 'forward' piaffe. If your cob responds by giving that lofty stride you know what to do – reward, reward and reward! In this way you can develop more and more strides in the passage and this, in and of itself, builds in transitions from piaffe into the passage. A word of warning, though: Ketchup often tried to go very deep and low in her outline when this exercise was introduced. Guard against this happening by observing closely what your cob does and responding appropriately. (When Ketchup went too deep, I raised my hands and increased the tone in my body.) Soon, you will be able to introduce this aiding from a more collected trot and I know that Ketchup didn't find the change of pace that initiates the passage too difficult. Developing passage sometimes out of the piaffe helps to keep a solid back and closed, engaged hind legs, while developing passage from the trot can help to produce a more forward rhythm and more expressive strides. Gradually, the two can be married together to produce an outstanding passage.

Canter pirouettes

The work leading towards the canter pirouette has also been mentioned in previous chapters. Here again, the feeling of having your cob up in front, high in the poll but soft in the mouth really does help. So, from a rounded outline in a collected canter, circle in a travers position, then simply raise both your hands slightly (the inside slightly higher) for a few moments while asking your cob to step a little with your outside leg, and guard against him speeding up by adding extra tone in your body and vibrating more on the outside rein. Wait until he has stepped a little more on the spot with his hind legs and is thus stepping round with his forehand. When this happens, stop and praise him before repeating the exercise. Just as in the piaffe, by maintaining this raised carriage you are guarding against him falling onto his forehand (and thus onto your hands), and also from dropping the impulsion already built into the canter.

Begin to build on the number of strides until you can ride six or eight strides of canter that make the full canter pirouette. Please don't practise this full form too much; always revert back to travers on small circles, as these strides are far less taxing and really guard against the hind legs cramping up and failing to step within the canter rhythm. (At the time of writing, Ketchup is only at the stage of practising a stride or two in the more collected, on-the-spot pirouette, but I'm sure she will build up to the full canter pirouette as long as I don't push things too fast.)

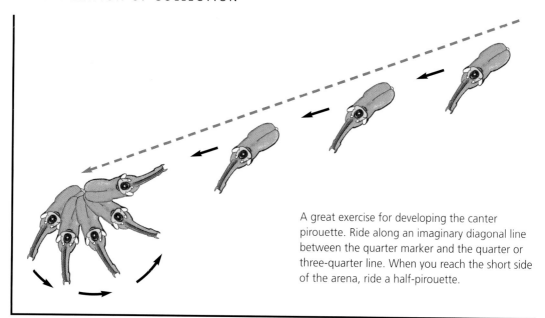

A great exercise for developing the canter pirouette. Ride along an imaginary diagonal line between the quarter marker and the quarter or three-quarter line. When you reach the short side of the arena, ride a half-pirouette.

In canter, turn down the three-quarter line and half-pass to the centre line or quarter line. When you reach that line, start a half-pirouette in canter.

Ride counter-canter along the wall, then incline off as though riding a tear-drop shape. When you have enough room, ride into travers position and complete a working half-pirouette in canter.

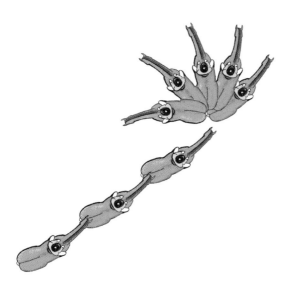

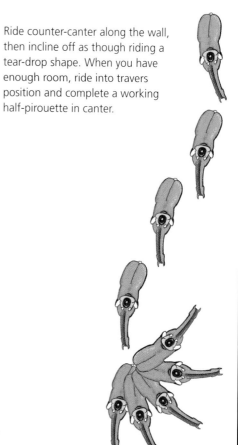

Exercises for developing the canter pirouette.

Once a few strides of canter pirouette are being offered, you can alter the exercises that you use to develop the canter pirouette. I like riding 'inverse' circles out of counter-canter in each of the corners (see diagram). To ride this exercise in counter-canter, incline a little off the track with the cob's hindquaters pushed a little towards the track, forehand to the inside and bend towards the wall. When you have enough room, begin your circle back to the track (and therefore true canter), with the quaters held in. This becomes a working pirouette. Another favourite exercise of mine is to half-pass in canter from the three-quarter line to the quarter-line, hold the quarters in as I turn the corner from the quarter-line back towards the quarter marker before half-passing once more to the centre line. (Again see the diagram.) Finally, an exercise which has worked well with Ketchup, is to ride shoulder-in along a diagonal line from the quarter marker to the quarter-line, canter pirouette round that corner to the opposite corner then canter straight back to the original corner marker across the diagonal.

Conclusion

I really hope that this text and its illustrations have shown just how versatile our humble cob can be. A friend of mine commented that this work really shows how trainable the cob actually is, and hopefully you will prove that Ketchup is not the exception. Happy riding... But one thing that I want to stress here is my main principle that hopefully says it all.

Although they are truly beautiful movements, piaffe, passage and canter pirouette, often thought of as the epitome of high-level equitation, are only as good as the preliminary exercises that precede them. A badly ridden piaffe or passage is of far less value and is far less classical than a beautifully balanced working trot, or a nicely active, rhythmical shoulder-in. It isn't the horse you ride that makes your training classical or correct; it is how you train him in those movements. The higher airs of canter pirouette are only the ends of your threads of training. You can follow those threads back to the first schooling sessions that aimed to develop balance, manoeuvrability, cadence and strength. Without our gentle methodology sad, turned-off and damaged equines will result. Give your cob his pride by using intelligent, classical, gentle methods that work *with* him rather than against him. Enjoy your schooling times and allow your cob to enjoy them too. Celebrate every achievement, every successful improvement in balance, every time things get easier. Celebrations really do give you a little encouragement – and this encouragement is felt no end by your cob.

Index